Getting into Medical School

SEVENTH EDITION

The Premedical Student's Guidebook
By Sanford J. Brown, M.D.

Director, Mendocino Foundation for Health Education

BARRON'S EDUCATIONAL SERIES, INC.
New York · London · Toronto · Sydney

All inquiries should be addressed to:
Barron's Educational Series, Inc.
250 Wireless Boulevard
Hauppauge, New York 11788

Library of Congress Catalog Card No. 89-6985
International Standard Book No. 0-8120-4266-2

Library of Congress Cataloging in Publication Data

Brown, Sanford Jay, 1946-
   Getting into medical school.

   Includes index.
   1. Medical colleges—United States—Admission.
2. Premedical education—United States. I. Title.
R838.4.B76   1989   610'.71'173   89-6985
ISBN 0-8120-4266-2

PRINTED IN THE UNITED STATES OF AMERICA

901   9770   987654321

this book is dedicated to
Sue, Gabriel, and Margot

Acknowledgments

My grateful appreciation to the premedical offices at University of California–Berkeley, University of Oregon–Eugene, and University of Wisconsin–Milwaukee for their helpful comments and for allowing me access to their materials. I am indebted to several of my teachers at the Medical College of Wisconsin: Dr. Sidney Shindell, for giving me the time, encouragement, and counsel in this project, and Dr. Walter Zeit for sharing with me his knowledge of pre- and post-Flexnerian medicine. I would especially like to thank Dr. David Nash for supplying much of the information that has been included in this revised version. My sincere thanks to Karen Levine for her marvelous illustrations. And to Gertrude Brown, my loving mother, who typed the original manuscript, and to Jill Hannum, who typed the final one.

Contents

PREFACE   *vii*

INTRODUCTION   *xi*

1 Choosing a College, Choosing a Major   1

It's not where you go to school or what you study, *1* The myth of the premedical major, *4* Getting "A's" in the sciences, *5* The physician as a scientist, *6* Abraham Flexner and his Flexner Report, *9* Emphasis on the sciences, *10* What kind of doctor do you want to become? *12* Avoid the extra science courses, *13*

2 The Premed Syndrome   17

The premedical mind, *17* The premedical society and the premedical adviser, *18* Not always an expert, *20* Did your adviser attend the convention? *23* Get acquainted . . . see what they write about you, *24* The premedical student, *28* The premedical syndrome, *29* A maniac in pursuit of medicine, *33* Failure is always a possibility, *34*

3 The New Medical College Admission Test (MCAT) 35

The most important criterion, *35* MCAT—a means for comparison, *36* MCAT scores, *38* How is it scored? *39* Preparing for the New MCAT, *41* Preparatory courses, *41*

4 Applying to a Medical School—When, Where, and How 45

How many applications? *45* Early decision, *48* Cost of applying, *49* Meeting the costs, *50* Minority students, *54* Are quotas legal? *56* Staying in can be harder than getting in, *59* Women students—another minority, *63* Special interest groups, *65* Making application—the AMCAS, *66* The transcripts, *67* What makes you different? *68* Recommendations, *72* The interview, *76*

5 How Medical School Admissions Committees Evaluate Applicants 85

Can the applicant make it? *86* Determining the motivation, *88*

6 Rejection and Your Alternatives 93

Rejection and reapplication, *93* Consider reapplying, *95* Foreign study, *99*

7 Summer Programs for the Premed 107

8 Directory of American Medical Schools 119

Index to U.S. Medical Schools 249

Preface

It's hard for me to believe that *Getting into Medical School* was first published fifteen years ago. When I wrote it, as a senior medical student in 1972–73, I had the motivation of wanting to tell my story—that of an atypical premed who had somehow made it into medical school—to other unusual applicants and aspirants. I remember writing the original manuscript almost nonstop in three weeks—in longhand! (This was before the era of word processing.) It was purely anecdotal. During the next year I added meat to the bones in the form of statistics, quotations, and other relevant data. In 1974, the first edition of *GIMS* was published. Now, I'm delighted to be writing yet another preface—this time for the seventh edition. Remaining in print for all these years makes me hope that not a few discouraged premeds have taken heart from my writing, persevered, and succeeded in their quests. I know that some have.

Traditionally, I have used the preface to bring my readers up to date on my professional activities and my attitudes and thoughts about medicine, and have usually ended with a heartening statement about what makes a good physician. I still like what I have said. To quote the first edition: "A professor of mine once said, 'What this country needs is fewer MDs and more physicians.' I believe what he meant was that we need more people to take care of the *whole* patient and not just his or her pathology. By that criterion, you don't have to be a great scientist to be a good physician. All you have to be is a good human being." And to quote the sixth: "Let each of you recognize the limits of health, the limits of your skill, and use creativity to find satisfaction in your healing art." Those sentiments still ring true for me; I find no need to change them.

What has changed, however, is the medical profession, and in some ways the change has been dramatic. In the past fifteen years, from when I first began to practice, we have seen a doctor shortage turn into, in some areas, a doctor glut. Malpractice premiums have risen precipitously and forced some practitioners either out of practice or into a different type of practice. There is much less physician autonomy as the solo practitioner is replaced by HMOs, PPOs, and IPAs, as well as other forms of group practice. And, on the other side of the equation, the applicant pool to medical schools has been declining for the past seven years. This has a lot of medical school deans and premedical advisors worried, as they fear that the caliber of the entering medical student may be declining. I, for one, do not share this concern.

Medicine has always attracted people with varied interests. Primarily, there is the desire to serve, to be useful, to make people better through our ministrations. But there is also the need for autonomy, for financial security, for continual busyness, and for mobility. For some people these needs are primary, and these are the people, I believe, who are now making alternative career choices, thereby reducing the applicant pool. What's left is still the stuff fine physicians are made of. Letters I've been receiving from discouraged premeds over the years convince me of it.

Since *GIMS* was first published, I've received hundreds of letters from my readers. Several years ago, I chose the best of them for a new book, *You Can Get into Medical School: Letters from Premeds*. Some represent fresh inquiries; others are follow-ups from earlier correspondences in which the aspirant either did or did not matriculate into a medical school. The successes and failures, as well as the personal and intimate premedical concerns expressed by readers of *GIMS*, formed a natural sequel to this book. *You Can Get into Medical School* is available through any bookstore or from the Mendocino Foundation for $8.50 postpaid.

Since writing the preface for the sixth edition, my work focus has changed. Always giving lip service to preventive medicine, I was finally able to actualize my concept of it through a program called *HealthTrends*. In it, we computer-track the changes in our patients' health over time and alert them when they become at risk for a disease. The idea is to suggest lifestyle changes to reverse abnormal trends, thus obviating a future need for medicine. The patient receives a full physical, as well as multiple computer printouts on his or her health. All of this information is incorporated into a chart which is the patient's to keep and bring back yearly for updating. In time we hope to accumulate enough of a database on each patient to show him or her graphic depictions of changing health patterns. *HealthTrends* gives substance to the ritual of the yearly physical and has been personally satisfying to me as well. Patients become more than a series of episodic diagnoses; they are seen as total individuals, and a clear picture of how their lifestyles influence their health emerges.

The computer will become, I predict, as important to the practice of medicine as the automobile and telephone. Not just an instrument for billing and sending timely reminders, the computer will revolutionize the way we practice. Artificial intelligence, data-basing, and interactive video are already making inroads into physicians' consciousness. Premeds need to become computer-literate. Fluency in Spanish won't hurt either. (Besides not learning how to play the piano, taking six years of high school and college French is the only other thing I rue.)

Despite the vagaries of economics, there will always be patients and there will always be physicians and other health-care workers to care for them. And no matter how much medicine changes, it will always offer its practitioners challenge, reward, and a sense of purposefulness. I continue to encourage altruistic and inquisitive spirits to choose a medical career. It remains a great profession.

I again welcome comments from readers. Should you wish to contact me, you may do so through the Mendocino Foundation, POB 1377, Mendocino, CA 95460.

Introduction

Again this year, almost twice as many premed students will apply to medical school as will be accepted. Even though the number of places in U.S. medical schools has risen steadily from 8,298 in 1960–61 to 13,697 in 1972–73 to 16,686 in 1987–88, there has been over a 150% increase in applicants for the same time period. Approximately 36,100 applicants sought entry in 1972–73, 36,700 in 1981–82, and 28,123 in 1987–88. It is anticipated that, although the number of applicants has begun to decrease, the number of students applying for the incoming classes of 1989–91 will continue to exceed 28,000. In 1967–68, 52% of applicants were admitted; in 1981–82, 47% were admitted; in 1987–88, 59% were admitted. Although things are getting better, these figures show that there simply are not enough places in the medical schools for all who have completed the premedical curriculum and are eager to become MDs.

I am not going to use this book to rant about the inequalities of the medical system or to suggest ways to increase medical manpower. We all know that the ideal is a place in medical school for every qualified applicant in a society in which medical schools are also subject to the principles of a free market economy. Instead, I am going to use this book to get you, the premedical student, *out* of the conventional and often erroneous ways of thinking about how to get into a medical school and *into* a more informed and advantageous position. After all, we haven't all had the same advantages, so this book will attempt to be an equalizer.

I am talking now of the premed dropout and the unsuccessful applicant: students from minority groups, borderline non-minority students, those with financial problems, women, students from colleges where there is no premedical adviser and, generally, students who, for one reason or another, have been discouraged from continuing in the premed curriculum. I am not writing for the student who wonders, "Do I really want to be a doctor?" There are enough banal books on that. This book is a survival kit, if you like, for the already committed. It is a step-by-step guide that anyone who wants to become a physician can put to use anywhere along the course of his or her premedical education. It will cover, from high school onward, the gamut of decision-making traumatic events that every premed must face, ranging from choosing a college and a major to accepting a medical school, and to what to do—short of suicide—if you are rejected by them all. Included are chapters on what it means to be a premed, the Medical College Admission Test, how to apply to medical schools, the way in which actual medical school admissions committees evaluate applicants, and finally, acceptance or rejection and your alternatives.

"Nothing is more boring than a science major with a 4.0 average."

Since medical schools cannot absorb more than 60% qualified applicants, it may seem paradoxical to take an interest in the students who either drop out of premed or are unsuccessful applicants. My feeling, simply, is that surviving the rigors of the premedical curriculum is not the most important prerequisite for becoming a good physician. Nothing is more boring to me than the science major with a 4.0 average who has done nothing but study and has pat replies to questions about why he or she wants to be a physician. Although a medical school's first concern in admitting applicants has traditionally been "Will they get through?" and not "What kind of physicians will they make?" I prefer to reverse this order of importance. I do not believe, for instance, that organic chemistry should be the most highly regarded academic experience of the premed. The reason that it is so regarded is that memorizing an organic chemistry textbook may simulate the most rigorous tasks of first- and second-year medical school, and medical school admissions committees feel that anyone who can handle it satisfactorily can pass basic medical sciences. Memorization may well be the last refuge of the unimaginative mind; nevertheless, the person with a capacity to absorb a lot of data will be favored by admissions committees over an individual who thinks more abstractly.

Basically I want to see a change in the profile of entering medical students so that creativity is valued over sheer stamina and sensitivity over callousness, so that there exists in the consciousness of the premedical student a recognition of the necessity for change, instead of an immutable conformity to the established ways of practicing medicine.

Encouragingly, times are changing. More and more applicants to medical schools are showing a variety of backgrounds which may include not only a nonscience major but an interim period in their education as well. Some have worked, others have traveled. Once having taken the required courses, nearly anyone who is otherwise qualified can go to medical school today.

There is room in medicine for all types of interests. Contrary to popular myth, every doctor is not a scientist who sees patients one minute and makes great scientific discoveries the next. In fact, not every doctor even sees patients. Some work for the Public Health Service tracking down sources of contagious disease; others are employed

"Memorization may be the last refuge of the unimaginative mind."

by state and local health departments to run immunization and multiphasic screening programs. Many doctors prefer teaching and academic medicine to private practice, and a few find satisfaction in editing medical journals and in medical illustration. There are currently fifty-odd specialties and sub-specialties in the area of medicine, and this number will certainly increase. In the future, more doctors will be involved in planning health care delivery systems on city, state, and federal levels. More young physicians will realize that preventing disease is easier than curing it and will come to consider health education, epidemiology, and community medicine as specialty fields. And with concern for our ecology increasing exponentially with time, environmental and industrial medicine and nutrition can be expected to attract more and more attention.

Medicine today can find a place for artists, photographers, educators, and historians. It needs biomedical engineers and computer programmers, administrators and basic research scientists. Medicine is the meeting ground of the arts and sciences. Its potential is limitless. It welcomes all kinds of people because diversity works against stagnation and aids growth. I mean to encourage all students to consider medicine as a career, not just the biologist, chemist, or physicist, but also the psychologist, sociologist, and economist, the anthropologist, journalist, and philosopher—and, of course, the poet.

CHAPTER 1

Choosing a College, Choosing a Major

Many people know early that they want to be physicians. Some have never wanted to be anything else. Others make their career choices in high school and in college. And there are the few who, like myself, decide on medicine after completing their college education. A sufficiently large number of students settle on medicine in high school to justify treating as the first order of business the choice of a college.

It's not where you go to school or what you study

It may come as news to some that the undergraduate institution attended carries little weight with medical schools. You can be accepted into medical school from virtually any accredited college or university, and your own academic credentials are vastly more important than

1

Many people know early that they want to be physicians.

the reputation of your school. It *is* true, however, that some undergraduate institutions are more successful than others at placing their graduates in medical schools. The student working the percentages in applying to college should ask to know the relative rather than the absolute number of graduates admitted to medical school from that institution during the preceding five years.

I suggest that it is foolish to see college merely as a stepping-stone to medical school. College can be a unique experience and a great deal more fun than graduate education. So choose your college for reasons other than its premedical program, which you can get anywhere. Attend a small school if you would prefer or a large school if you want anonymity or an active campus life. Accept a school with an outstanding English or theatre arts and drama department. Go to a region of the country where you have never been before. Take your junior year abroad. Experiment.

Remember that once you become a doctor, your patients won't care where you went to college.

People won't even care where you attended medical school or ask about the grades you earned or if you graduated with honors. They will only be concerned that you understand them and their medical problems. So if you use your college years to broaden your base of experience, in the long run you'll be doing your patients a service.

The myth of the premedical major

Wherever you go there are, of course, the exigencies of the premedical program, and I do mean to talk about them. First, however, let us explode once and for all the myth of the premedical major. You cannot go to college and major in premed. Following a premed curriculum means nothing more than taking some basic science courses required by most medical schools. Minimum requirements are usually one year of general biology, one year of physics, one year each of inorganic and organic chemistry. Other required subjects vary with the school and may include English, mathematics, calculus, and other more specialized science courses.

Medical schools always look at an applicant's science and nonscience cumulative grade point average, with emphasis on the science GPA (into which math grades are averaged). This has numerous implications; for if you are a nonscience major, each science course you take will have a considerable effect on your science average, whereas those majoring in science can do poorly in one course without any devastating effect. On the other hand it is true that science is a tougher major than either the humanities or social sciences, and science majors applying to medical schools have lower overall cumulative averages than their nonscience major counterparts. What follows from all of this?

> *Majoring in a nonscience will probably raise your overall GPA and put you in a more advantageous position when seeking admission to a medical college.*

Medical school admission committees today welcome the applicant who did not major in science. However, they must be sufficiently impressed with your premedical course grades to admit you.

Getting "A's" in the sciences

How, then, can you do well in the required sciences? In the first place, do not make the mistake that many premeds make. I always hear students say that a grade of "C" from school X is the equivalent of a "B" from school Y or of an "A" from school Z. This is pure myth. An "A" goes down as an "A" and a "B" as a "B." There are no conversion factors in evaluating applicants' grades from different schools. So if a required premed course is ridiculously hard, or the competition is especially rough, and science is not your bag, then do yourself a favor and take the course somewhere else. This is extremely important, since many medical schools will not even look at your application unless you have a B+ (3.3–3.5) average or better in science, as well as overall.

The extremes to which some universities may go to "keep students competitive" is astounding. My own undergraduate school is a case in point. It had early achieved a reputation as a science school, although it had excellent liberal arts departments. Naturally, it attracted many science students—far more, in fact, than it had the faculty or facilities to train. Most of the influx wanted to concentrate in biology, although physics and chemistry also received more people than they could comfortably handle. The situation was somewhat tolerable at the lower course levels but would have become cataclysmic if all students had been permitted to advance to their junior and senior years with normal attrition rates. To ease matters, all students intending to major in biology and physics, as well as in engineering, were routed first through freshman inorganic chemistry along with all the budding chemists. "Into the valley of death rode the six hundred," including the premeds. I was so intimidated by my school's science department that I waited for the Department of Earth and Space Sciences to open its doors before I dared fulfill my university's science requirements. When I finally did take premed inorganic chemistry it was in night school at a local community college.

I do not mean to suggest that your professors are out to fail you, but some departments do believe in making things purposely difficult, for reasons of either pride or practicality. My advice is simply not to bother with them. Take that inorganic or organic chemistry course in summer school. Don't get hassled.

The physician as a scientist

The emphasis that has been placed on the basic sciences in recent years has given many people the erroneous impression that all doctors are scientists. This is simply untrue, but the evolution of the idea is an interesting bit of medical history. At this point it might be helpful to examine it and see how the idea of physician as scientist has evolved and influenced medical school admission policies during recent years.

The first medical schools in this country were those associated with established universities such as Harvard, the University of Pennsylvania and the University of Maryland. These schools were, for their day, reasonably substantial medical schools with high academic standards.

During the years of the great immigration to this country, many of the newcomers already had a European medical degree while others wished to study medicine in the European tradition after they arrived. In Europe, a physician who had attained any degree of eminence was called "professor." A European who became sick did not go to a practitioner, specialist, or consultant but to a professor at some medical center. When an immigrant became sick, he or she, too, wanted to go to a professor. It was part of the European heritage. However, in most states there were no medical schools and consequently no professors.

It wasn't long before groups of physicians began to band together and start medical schools of their own. Probably one of the motives behind this was that these doctors could then hold professorships in their own medical schools, thereby acquiring the title of professor. This type of school, known as the proprietary medical school, was organized for prestige and profit and flourished until 1906, when there were about 160 medical schools in this country. With the exception of those affiliated with the older universities, all the rest were proprietary schools.

". . . when enrollments dropped, professors went out to solicit students."

In most cases these proprietary schools had low academic standards and sometimes admitted students without a high school education. Virtually anyone was admitted who could pay the tuition, and when enrollment dropped, the professors went out to solicit students. There were no state agencies to regulate the practice of medicine. Persons attending proprietary schools, as well as those attending some major universities, spent two years after high school studying medicine and two summers of preceptorship with local practitioners. With this meager background students went out to practice. Licensure requirement was that the student merely have graduated from any of the medical schools then existent.

Abraham Flexner and his Flexner Report

By the turn of the century, the Carnegie Foundation for the Advancement of Teaching, which had been engaged in activities to improve the quality of teaching in general, employed Abraham Flexner, who was not a physician, to make a survey of medical education in the United States. In 1909 Flexner personally visited every medical school in this country and evaluated the schools on the basis of their requirements for admission, the caliber of their faculty, and the quality of their laboratories and physical facilities. When he finished, he formulated the now famous *Flexner Report*, which was published by the Carnegie Foundation in 1910.

In this report, medical schools were classified as A-, B-, or C-type schools. Many of the medical schools then operating received a C rating. All of those rated C were proprietary type schools. Following the *Flexner Report*, the states established boards of medical examiners and passed medical practice acts. These boards instituted examinations for medical licensure and said, in effect, that a person was not eligible to take the exam unless that person had graduated from a Class A school. This immediately put the Class B and Class C schools out of business, so that by 1920 there were only 72 medical schools left in the United States.

It was recommended in the *Flexner Report* that medical schools, in order to qualify for Class A rating, become affiliated with universities which could provide the student with a reasonable academic background and good laboratory facilities. Requirements for admission to medical school quickly included a year of liberal arts education after high school. As time went on it was recognized that, as knowledge in all fields increased, more preparation was necessary.

Gradually admissions requirements were changed from one to two years of college, from two to three years, and finally to four years.

Today all medical schools prefer that applicants have a bachelor's degree and some require it.

Emphasis on the sciences

Another change occurred. As emphasis for admission to medical school was placed more and more heavily on the scientific disciplines, premedical programs in the liberal arts colleges came to center around comparative vertebrate anatomy, general biology, physics, and chemistry. By the 1930s the broad liberal arts education fostered by the old premedical programs was subdued almost totally by scientific training. This attitude lasted until after World War II. Then, in the late forties and early fifties, medical schools began to encourage applicants to take a fourth year and use it to study the humanities. For a short while students began choosing nonscience majors. Few who wanted to go to medical school intended careers in full-time scientific research or academic medicine.

In the late fifties the wheel again came full circle. There was an explosion in scientific and technical information beginning with Russia's Sputnik in 1957. Suddenly vast amounts of money became available for research. Medical schools, supported by government grants, hired more faculty for full-time research positions. Aided by government money, medical schools expanded their laboratories in the basic sciences. Less attention was paid to community medical care and medical schools began to favor students who had majored in biology or chemistry, with preference given to those who had taken higher level courses. Premeds responded by studying the more advanced and more difficult sciences, resulting in an upgrading of the preparation of the matriculating medical student. The model for this generation of students became the academic physician who spent 70% of his or her time in research and 30% in patient care.

The situation remained unchanged until the mid-sixties when a large number of students in the physical sciences began to apply to medical school with the intent of becoming biomedical engineers. It was the era of the pacemaker and other spectacular technical solutions to medical problems. Then in 1968 the picture changed again. The majority of young people had turned against the Vietnam War, the poor were becoming increasingly visible, and the inequities in the American way of life stood out glaringly. Premedical students responded by becoming family physicians rather than specialists. Many of today's graduates are attracted to the subspecialties that have burgeoned from the technological advances of the last decade—angiography and angioplasty, CT scanning and nuclear magnetic resonance imaging, organ transplants, and the medical laser, as well as computer applications to the medical sciences.

What kind of doctor do you want to become?

With myriad alternatives in a medical career, the issue of what to major in is more a question of what type of physician you wish eventually to become. If you want a life of medical research, by all means enter medical school with a strong background in the basic sciences. If your interests in medicine are more social, however, then ten years hence an undergraduate major in sociology or economics will probably be more advantageous to you than one in biology or chemistry. And if, like most entering college students, you are undecided, then major in whatever turns you on. Do you think you'd like a major in music or drama? Does the study of anthropology intrigue you? Would you mind four years of reading great literature or sculpting, drawing or painting? Do these things! As long as you take the required premedical courses, no college major will handicap you or make you less prepared to perform adequately in medical school. And where except in college will you ever again have the chance to study Chaucer, Egyptian hieroglyphics, or pre-Socratic philosophy? College is your opportunity to develop your full potential; use it just for that. Medical school will give you all the science you will ever need to be a competent physician, I assure you. Do not waste your time choosing a science major if you are unhappy with one or taking any science course that will be duplicated in the medical curriculum.

For the 1987–88 entering class, students who majored in one of the physical sciences had the highest rate of acceptance to medical school. However, nonscience majors—in fields such as economics and philosophy—had an acceptance rate higher than those who majored in the biological sciences (63.8% vs. 57.5%). English majors had a 70.7% acceptance rate! Interestingly, those who majored in other health professions, such as pharmacy or nursing, had the lowest acceptance rate—45.8%.

Again I urge you to concentrate in any area that is of genuine interest to you. No major yields a significantly higher percentage of successful applicants, nor can any be singled out as a barrier to medical school admission.

Avoid the extra science courses

I often hear undergraduates talk about taking science courses that will "help" them in medical school, by which I suppose they mean courses in biochemistry, physiology, comparative anatomy, and the like. It is true that those courses may make the first year of medical school somewhat easier. However, the degree of simplicity of the course must also be seen as directly proportional to the amount of boredom it generates. Coming to med school with an English major, I found my first year truly difficult but quite fascinating, because everything I learned was new to me.

Unless you have a genuine interest in scientific material, you are not necessarily doing yourself a favor by taking extra science courses.

This is only logical. In the first place you always do one thing at the expense of another. That course in statistics may mean passing up the one in creative writing offered by the novelist in residence at your university. Second, the way a course is taught at one school may be totally unrelated to the way it is handled at another. For example, the freshman biochemistry course at my medical school was so far out that former biochemistry majors had difficulty passing it. Third, medical schools may not care how many science courses you have taken as long as you have met their requirements and they are convinced you can do medical school work. In addition, some medical schools may not accept credit earned in these courses.

What undergraduates fail to understand about medical school is that with diligence and perseverance anyone with average intelligence can pass through it successfully.

The hardest obstacle to overcome in becoming a physician is getting admitted to a medical school.

About 40% of those applicants considered fully qualified are rejected, whereas less than 2% of any entering class fails to graduate, and most of these failures are for nonacademic reasons. A friend of mine is fond of asking, "What do they call the person who graduates last in his medical school class?" The answer, of course, is "doctor."

I believe that performance in premedical courses, on the Medical College Admissions Test, or even during the first two years of medical school is no indication of the kind of physician you will become. Your success as a practitioner is more a function of your personality, character, and native intelligence than of your grades. Medicine has always been more of an art than a science. Science is but one of the tools the doctor uses to deliver total care to the patient. It is not the only tool.

"Science is but one of the tools the doctor uses to deliver total care to the patient."

CHAPTER **2**

The Premed Syndrome

Once you have decided to opt for medicine you become a premed. It's that simple. It has nothing to do with joining a premedical club or acquiring a premedical adviser. Nor is it required that you be attending a college or university. It all has to do with consciousness.

The premedical mind

Being premed is a state of mind. Some people know when they're five, with their first chemistry set or doctor's bag. A friend of mine became a definite premed at age twelve, when his father gave him a copy of Gray's *Anatomy*— unabridged. While I was in college the last thing I thought to become was a doctor, so I wasn't a premed until after I graduated.

A study of the birth dates of the 1987–88 applicant pool

showed that 59% were less than 24 years old, as compared with percentages of 64 to 68% in the mid-1970's. However, as is often the case, the students in this age group had the highest percentage of acceptance. Although there is a generally declining acceptance rate for applicants over 24, it is notable that the acceptance rate for older applicants has increased in recent years. For the 1987–88 entering class, 40% of applicants 32 to 37 years old and 34% of those 38 and over were accepted to medical school.

Since all medical schools require completion of at least three years of college, and prefer four, before they will admit you, there is not much an ambitious high school student can do except bide time. There are special six-year programs for high school seniors leading to the combined BA or BS and MD degrees, such as those at Boston University and Northwestern, but these are highly competitive. If you're not in any hurry to become a doctor, I would advise spending four years in college and using your senior year for electives to take something other than premedical science courses. Many doctors who spent only three years in college often mourn the loss of that fourth year.

The premedical society and the premedical adviser

Once you are a matriculated college student your school may offer facilities and services to assist you. Notably, there will be a premedical club and a premedical adviser. Regarding the former, I can offer the words of Marx (Groucho, not Karl), who said that he would not belong to any club that would accept him as a member. Apart from their annual pilgrimage to a medical school (a trip which you can more profitably make on your own), the value of such clubs is dubious. Joining the club may even make you up tight, since you will be seeing the same people you regularly compete with in your premedical courses.

Medical schools couldn't care less if you were a member of the premedical society.

It makes no sense for you to join because you think it will look impressive on your record. Also, it is important to remember that these societies are clubs sponsored by the students and are not considered a service of the university. On the other hand, the premedical adviser is a service of the university and ignoring the adviser would be foolhardy, as he or she can be critical to your case.

My own premedical adviser, after hearing my story, asked me what I was going to do when I didn't get into medical school. Fortunately, I was obsessed with the idea of becoming a doctor, and since he didn't give me the encouraging counsel I wished to hear, I simply did not hear him. The question of whether his advice was good advice never entered my mind.

However, when I first realized that his position had no job description I began to wonder about the premedical

I took it on blind faith that the premedical adviser knew his business.

adviser's credentials and experience and about what exactly he could do for me that I couldn't do for myself. What follows is a profile of the premedical adviser which answers these questions and may also answer some others that you perhaps have.

Not always an expert

First off, premedical advisers are rarely, if ever, physicians themselves. They are almost always faculty members at the university who have taken an interest in the plight of the premedical student or have simply been appointed to the job. Although premedical advisers can be members of any department, they are most frequently from the science faculty. At most places, the job is part time and the adviser puts in a few mornings or afternoons a week without extra pay.

The majority of schools have one premedical adviser; some have more than one, and others have none at all. In the latter case the faculty itself assumes the role of adviser to the premed students. In many places, serving as the premedical adviser takes the place of having to serve on other faculty committees or on the faculty senate. Since success among the teaching staff is often judged to be inversely proportional to the amount of time a faculty

"Premedical advisers are rarely, if ever, doctors themselves."

member spends with students, it is not incorrect to say that the position of premedical adviser is not terribly sought after. As with most academic committee work, the term of a premedical adviser may be surprisingly short. One adviser may serve for quite a long time and then (possibly in the middle of your own college career) relinquish the post to a fresh recruit. It is important for the student to know how long the adviser has held that post so that it will be possible to evaluate accordingly the advice rendered. Experience at this job is of key importance.

Some advisers, like some teachers, keep only one step ahead of their students.

As there is no required formal educational process for advisers to go through before they assume their position, it is very difficult for a student to assess the adviser's competence. The premedical adviser holds no degree or certification for the job, is not licensed, and is not subject to peer review. The adviser is only as good as personal interest and involvement allow.

An Association of Advisors for the Health Professions does exist. It is a loosely structured organization holding yearly regional meetings for the Northeast, Southeast, Western and Central states. Although many premedical advisers belong to this organization, not all attend the yearly meeting in their region. The meeting offers a sort of refresher course on the state of education in the health professions and gives the advisers a chance to have their questions answered by the medical school admissions people who attend, as well as to make personal contacts. Matters taken up at the meeting may include how to write an evaluation for a student applying to medical school, current trends in admissions, and up-to-date information on the MCAT.

Did your adviser attend the meeting?

This organization does offer its members a quarterly journal, called *The Advisor*. This publication, together with the yearly regional meetings and one national meeting of the association, constitutes the prime opportunities for premed advisers to keep up in the field. In 1987 I attended the Western Regional Meeting at Asilomar, California. I was impressed with the agenda and also with the dedication and sincerity of the premedical advisers that I met.

My advice to you is to find out if your premed adviser belongs to this association. If he or she does not, then look for someone who does. This, in addition to experience, is the best way to judge your adviser's reliability. Most premedical advisers will talk to you even if you're not a student at their college, so don't be shy about calling up and asking for an appointment.

The question arises, "What can my premedical adviser tell me that I don't already know?" In truth, it may not be very much. The core of the premedical adviser's knowledge comes from two publications that are readily available to the public. They are *Medical School Admission Requirements* and the new American Association of Medical Colleges application forms which include some valuable information on each of the participating schools. In addition, the adviser receives a newsletter, published by the AAMC, which may have occasional nuggets of information. A very helpful publication is the *Journal of the American Medical Association*, which can be found in most libraries. Each year this journal gives a complete profile of the entering freshman class to medical school. Included are the number of applications and applicants, their GPAs, average MCAT scores, the number accepted and rejected, and pertinent analyses of factors affecting medical school admissions. As far as printed matter is concerned, you can probably lay your hands on as much stuff as your adviser. If you don't feel like digging up your own information, you should feel free to ask your adviser if you can peruse the office files. As far as I know, there are no secret documents there, so I see no reason for objection.

Certainly your adviser can provide valuable help, and if yours is conscientious you may not even have need of this book. Most of the things I talk about—i.e., choosing a major, taking the MCAT, applying to medical school, and facing alternatives—should be covered adequately by your adviser during your four years as an undergraduate. One of the functions of this book is to serve as a primary adviser for students who have no one at their school and to offer a second opinion for those dissatisfied with what they have already been told.

Get acquainted . . . see what they write about you . . .

Now, even if your premed adviser is abominable, it is most important to get acquainted—whether or not you take any advice—because most medical schools require

"Even if your premedical adviser is abominable . . ."

a letter of recommendation from the premedical committee, which may be made up wholly or in part by the premedical adviser.

Later we will talk about the kinds of recommendations faculty members may write. It is important for students to remember, however, that in most cases these recommendations are not sent directly to the medical schools to which you have applied. The premedical committee drafts and sends a composite letter. Though your professors may describe you in the most glowing terms, the *tone* of the committee's letter will clearly depend on how well you are known to the person drafting it—usually the premedical adviser.

The following are two actual letters from premedical committees. They appeared in an issue of *The Advisor* which reported on a symposium of letters of evaluation sponsored by the Western Association of Advisors for the Health Professions. The presentation from which these two letters are excerpted was made by Dr. John P. Steward of the Stanford University School of Medicine. The comments following the letters are Dr. Steward's.

FIRST LETTER:

Premedical Adviser:

Not much need to add to underscore the fact that .... is a gem. I enjoyed my first encounter with this very bright lad three years ago when, as a freshman who had already traveled abroad as far as .... and .... he was then plowing through all kinds of advanced courses, displaying the energy and enormous enthusiasm which were to mark every step of his journey through .... He had come to college imbued with the drive to become a doctor from the earliest age and with the simplest of explanations: "I just want to be able to help people." His next greatest ambition

was to get back to Europe, to get to know people; and he has
done every kind of menial labor, even jerking sodas, to earn
the money. Sure enough, the next summer found him working
for .... in ...., and now he has only just returned
from the greatly enriching experience of a junior year abroad
where he was registered in school exactly the same as
.... students, not as a foreigner, in an experimental
center in ...., a development of the University of
.........., but the cosmopolitan life has in no way diminished
his single-minded concentration on becoming a physician.
Furthermore, it is perfectly clear that here is a young man
who has pursued the epitome of the liberal arts program not
in the least with any idea of minimizing the sciences, as his
very high standing in all the required courses testify—he is
only saving them up for medical school! It is not possible that
we will be presenting a stronger or more engaging candidate
this year—a star.

COMMENTS ON LETTER:

The helpful parts of the letter were . . . the way the
premedical adviser summarized his candidate. This excellent
letter is typical of letters coming from this academically
excellent institution.

SECOND LETTER:

Premedical Adviser:
.... is enrolled in the premedical curriculum of this
University and is applying for admission to your School of
Medicine. He is expected to graduate with a Bachelor's
Degree in June, 1971.

At the present time, ...'s cumulative grade point
average is 3.64.

The premedical faculty of the College of Science acts as a
committee to pass on applicants for recommendation to
medical school. After due consideration of his case, the five
members of .... committee were unanimous in recom-
mending him as an excellent candidate.

One committee member commented that he had a pleasant

*personality—on the quiet side—and would expect him to be
in the upper half of his class.*

*The possible ratings given to applicants who receive the
recommendations of the Committee are: not recommended,
fair candidate, good candidate, excellent candidate.*

COMMENTS ON LETTER:

This is an instance where we have no choice but to say here
is a student that, as far as we are concerned, we don't care
what his G.P.A. is, and we don't want to know anything else
about him if this is all the premedical adviser could say.

Again, we will interpret what you write in light of the fact
that we assume you have done your best.

Once you have developed a personal relationship with
your adviser you can be sure that the letter of evaluation
will show the admissions committees that you're more
than just a cipher. Whether or not the adviser knows how
to write a good letter of evaluation is something you can
do very little about, so don't worry about it.

The premedical student

Having discussed the premedical adviser, the next order
of business is the premedical student. What do other
people see in him or her? What is the student's self-
image?

Peer group evaluations usually label premed students
"grade-grubbers," "gunners," or "greasers" depending on
the part of the country they come from. Other disparaging
adjectives used for the premed are ruthless, antisocial,
narrow-minded, insincere, cutthroat, dull, and brown-
nose. On the other hand, students who see the premeds
more as a benign than as a malignant force have described
them as idealistic, dedicated, and brilliant.

Among faculty members the premedical student is

usually highly regarded. Unfavorable comments from this group are that premeds are more concerned with grades than subject matter and are not fully interested in participation in the whole college experience. On the favorable side, professors often remark that premeds are desirable students who make many contributions to the extracurricular program of their colleges.

What of the premed's own self-image? Certainly many students exhibit elitist tendencies—all the more so the longer they remain premeds. Others, for whom the curriculum is an ordeal, see what they are sacrificing in time and may actually feel relatively deprived when comparing themselves with their classmates. Still others may have no self-image at all connected with being premed. In the true democratic spirit, they do not see themselves as fundamentally different from their peers. At the core though, if the premed is being motivated by a desire to aid others, by a need for self-gratification, for financial security, or for power, prestige, knowledge, or a challenging and varied career, that student is likely to feel good about what he or she is doing and to have a positive self-image. If, however, the student has an unsatisfied, subliminal yearning to be a physical education teacher, but a parent in the medical profession is calling all the shots, then that student is not going to be very happy as a premed or in medical school.

The premedical syndrome

For those who don't genuinely want to become doctors, the premed curriculum, not to mention medical school, will be sheer hell. To those at peace with themselves it can be a joy. Yet some students who genuinely want to

"The premed's self-image."

study medicine are not at all at peace with themselves, and they let the rigors of the premed curriculum interfere with their self-development. They suffer from what I call the premedical syndrome.

The affliction is readily diagnosed. On any college campus, those suffering from the premed syndrome are the students who look as if they've been in a pressure cooker. Worn and haggard, but very determined, they are the last to leave the library at night and the first to arrive in the morning. They don't go out much, unless there's a lecture on diabetes or heart disease. Their extracurricular activities consist of membership in the premedical society and flipping a Frisbee for physical fitness. Artistically, all of their drawing is done with a number two lead pencil on IBM sheets. Musically, they are satisfied with AM radio. Ask them to demonstrate or sign a petition, and they say, "What, and blow med school?!" Psychologically, they are anal retentive types who make up daily schedules so they won't forget anything.

Their lab notebooks are impeccably neat. Major headings are underlined in red, minor ones in blue.

They never miss a class without getting the notes. All homework assignments are handed in on time. Before

"Worn and haggard, they are the last to leave the library at night and the first to arrive in the morning."

examinations they study incessantly, develop a tachycardia and become diaphoretic. This anxiety is theoretically linked with an impending sense of doom, but the symptoms promptly abate after they "ace," "gun," or are "all over" the exam. If they do poorly they are miserable and hard to live with.

The syndrome is marked by exacerbations (failures) and remissions (successes), culminating in a crisis (acceptance or rejection). The individual may recover completely (is accepted), be left with permanent residual damage (is rejected), or may pass into a carrier state (reapplies again the next year).

A maniac in pursuit of medicine

This was written in gross caricature, of course. All the same it is not hard to see why the premed is maniacal in the pursuit of medicine. In our society the premedical student runs a particular risk and has far more to lose than any other preprofessional. Of all the professions, none turns away qualified applicants as frequently as does medicine. In addition, one-quarter of your college career will be spent taking courses which, should you complete them successfully, will serve only to qualify you for admission into a medical school. Contrast this situation to law, for which no specific academic preparation is required of aspiring students.

The premedical student may have majored in science with no intention of becoming a scientist or studied literature without any desire to teach. The primary goal is medicine, and unless prepared for the possibility of not gaining admission to professional school, the student may have nothing at all on which to fall back.

Failure is always a possibility

The sad fact is that the students who are not admitted
have most probably lost out not because they are at fault
but because the system cannot absorb them, even though
they may be competent, sincere, and dedicated. There
are alternatives for the rejected applicants, and I will be
talking about them later; however, *the ambitious pursuit
of medical school acceptance is not a guarantee of success.*
If you are prepared to make the commitment and to cope
with possible failure (and I hope that you are) then read
on. Otherwise, if you haven't already marked up the
pages, see if you can't get some money back at the
bookstore.

CHAPTER 3

The New Medical College Admission Test (MCAT)

The most important criterion

Besides your GPA there is, probably, no single more important criterion for admission to medical school today than your performance on the Medical College Admission Test. Since it is hard for admissions committees to rate one college against another, the MCAT provides a standard by which all candidates may be compared. The MCAT is a standardized factor, one path in the admissions process that everyone must follow. Virtually all schools require you to report your MCAT scores.

Now, if you have been anything other than a superior undergraduate student, the MCAT is for your benefit. It is your chance to show off and show up all those compulsive premeds who study incessantly and give you a guilty conscience for going out and having a good time. Even if you have a borderline GPA, high scores on this exam will indicate to medical schools that you have the potential to do work that will be up to their standards. On the other hand, low MCAT scores from a student with a high GPA might indicate someone who has reached his or her limits in college and may not be able to handle the more difficult work load of medical school.

After all, don't you spend countless hours studying to boost your grade point? How much time have you spent to assure yourself high scores on this all important test? It is a fact that your performance on this six-hour exam will help or hurt you as much as that GPA you sweated for during your entire college career.

MCAT—a means for comparison

By now I hope you are wondering why the MCAT is of such great consequence and what you can do to be ready for it. To begin with, you must realize that in selecting applicants medical schools are eternally looking for the single most consistent predictor of medical school success. In the past, success has correlated most reliably with GPA, but using grade points has caused two major problems. One, which we have already mentioned, is that grades are not always comparable from college to college. The attempt to adjust grades (after the initial screening— before it, no adjustments are made, and an "A" is an "A" wherever it was earned) is informal at best. Admissions committees may err at the extremes, either by assuming more differences between schools than actually exist, or by not accepting the fact that colleges actually do differ in their academic standards.

The second difficulty with grade points has emerged

more recently. During the past few years a side effect of student protest has been a modification of the grading system at many universities, with evaluations replacing letter grades as a more meaningful way to assess a student's ability. Indeed, this pass-fail trend has been adopted by medical schools, with the result that many have done away with class rankings and today operate exclusively on a satisfactory-unsatisfactory grading system. At this point, however, medical schools feel justified in using nonletter grades because, by the process of selection, they have prejudged the student to be capable of becoming a physician and see little advantage in continuing to foster a competitive atmosphere. On the undergraduate level these changes may be beneficial to the students seeking self-improvement, but they have made the task of selecting among applicants to medical school increasingly difficult. The problem is compounded by teachers who have become disenchanted with the traditional grading system and have performed as their small protest the existential act of giving all their students "A's."

Medical school admissions committees must consider whether the grade itself is a valid measure of the applicant's performance. If the applicant presents a "pass" instead of a letter grade, the task of evaluation is that much harder, since what constitutes satisfactory completion of the course is usually not described on the transcript.

When admissions committees finally do lose faith in the GPA as a means of selecting students who are bright enough to graduate from a school of medicine, there will be only one objective criterion left—the MCAT. It will be the last bastion of objectivity left to the medical school, the only means by which applicants may be differentiated in an impartial manner.

MCAT scores

Let us examine for a moment the way the MCAT is presently set up and scored. Starting with the test administered in the spring of 1977, the MCAT is completely new. The old test consisting of four categories (Science, Math, Vocabulary and General Information) has been entirely rewritten. This is how the New MCAT looks.

First, the exam is now twice as long as the old test. There are two sessions (morning, four hours; afternoon, three hours) with a one-hour lunch break.

Secondly, there are several sections on the exam that are new and unique for the MCAT. Part One of the test is titled Scientific Knowledge. This section is subdivided into questions dealing with biology, chemistry, and physics. There are 38 biology, 49 chemistry, and 38 physics questions in a 135-minute time period. These types of questions are all multiple-choice and factual in content. They are the usual standard fare science questions covering information from introductory-level college courses.

Part Two of the New MCAT consists of 66 intermingled biology, chemistry, and physics questions under the heading of Science Problems. This section takes about 85 minutes. The questions in Part Two are more challenging than those in Part One because they are presented in sets. Each set contains a problem developed around two or more scientific concepts or principles. You may be asked to infer some information or to make a judgment based on a short reading passage.

Part Three of the exam begins immediately after lunch and consists of 68 reading questions given in an 85-minute period. This part is known as Skills Analysis: Reading.

Again, a short passage dealing with a scientific subject will be presented and several multiple-choice questions will follow.

Part Four of the exam is called Skills Analysis: Quantitative. This part also has 68 questions and a duration of 85 minutes. Here, reading passages will deal with graphs, charts, and other data, and you will be asked to interpret the information provided.

How is it scored?

According to the official AAMC *New MCAT Student Manual,* six separate scores will be presented to the candidate who completes the test. Separate scores indicate your performance for 1) Biology, 2) Chemistry, 3) Physics, 4) Science Problems, 5) Skills Analysis: Reading, and lastly 6) Skills Analysis: Quantitative. Your Biology score combines the biology questions in Science Knowledge with the biology questions in Science Problems. Scores in Chemistry and Physics are computed similarly.

According to the *Student Manual,* "your total score is a reflection of your right answers only. This means that a wrong answer will be scored exactly the same as a no answer." In other words, do not leave any space blank; answer every single question, even if you have to guess. You will not be penalized, so the best policy is to fill in every answer space. This is crucial to remember.

The scores are reported on a new scale ranging from 1 (lowest) to 15 (highest). Raw scores that you get are converted to a score on the 15-point scale. Let's say you get 42 out of 60 questions correct on one section; this would probably convert to an 11 or 12 on the new scale. In this manner, even though there might be a slight

"Answer every single question, even if you have to guess."

difference in the raw scores among several students, their interval score (1 to 15) will be the same.

Preparing for the New MCAT

To the question "Can I prepare for the MCAT?" the answer is an emphatic YES. Some of the ways to prepare are obvious, and you probably already know them. If you are at all conscientious, you may already have purchased one of the books that have questions simulating the MCAT. Those I have seen pattern their questions after the actual MCAT and should give you a good idea of what to expect. A few tips—start using these books early (not a week before the exam) and look up the things you do not know. Get into a routine of doing a number of pages or questions each day and stick to it. This kind of discipline, incidentally, will also get you through medical school.

It is a very good idea to take this exam as seriously as you took organic chemistry. If need be, pretend that the MCAT is simply another premed course in which you must do well in order to get into medical school. It would be wise to start your systematic review procedure about six months before you plan to take the real thing. Get "psyched" early and build up your confidence so that you can perform really well on the test.

Preparatory courses

There is currently much controversy surrounding the merits of taking a special prep or cram course for the New MCAT exam. Inasmuch as these types of commercial courses are expensive and time-consuming, you really have to be seriously committed to doing well on the exam.

However, the MCAT preparation centers can help you prepare for the exam in one very important way—building confidence. If you've paid good money for a course (money that you would have used for a new turntable!) then you will force yourself to study and review your notes. In this manner you will increase your confidence because of a sense of preparation and knowing that you are not facing the test cold. If you are confident in your own performance this will decrease the anxiety level that accompanies the MCAT and your scores are bound to be higher. Remember, it is a two-way street. The prep courses won't help you if you don't give the necessary hours to review and to do practice problems.

Lastly, save all your notes and tests from the important science courses. In this way you will be able to review your own material and look over your review sheets from previous study binges. Why waste all of that work that you had to do anyway? Good students keep their notes in binders or folders so that they are still legible a year or two later. It wouldn't hurt to retake some of your class tests as practice to help point out to yourself areas in which you may need some extra work.

The major preparatory courses are offered in most cities. The local offices of these commercial centers can be found in the yellow pages, or just ask around at your college and you will be surprised at how many people have taken the course themselves. In other words, you also should keep your eyes and ears open about what is going on at your school and what the going rates are for such courses.

Before leaving the subject of the MCAT, I must take up two frequently asked questions: "When should I take the MCAT?" and "When is it necessary to take it more than once?" There is no doubt in my mind that the New

MCAT should first be taken in the spring of your junior year. Unless you plan to pick up a summer course, the additional time afforded by taking the exam in the fall will not be a distinct advantage. In fact, you will lose a great deal of momentum. By taking the New MCAT in the spring, you will have your scores by summer, and you can begin to apply to medical schools June 15 for AMCAS schools and often earlier for non-AMCAS schools. However, if you wait until the fall of your senior year to take it, your scores won't be processed until November (it takes six weeks to score the MCAT), and medical schools won't have them until December or, possibly, early January. By that time, most of your premedical friends will have already gone for their interviews, and quite a few may have been accepted by a medical school. This will do little to lessen your anxiety. So unless there are unusual circumstances (e.g., you decide in your senior year to become a premed), take the New MCAT in the spring. Of course, candidates for early admission to medical school (after three years of college) should take the exam in the fall of their junior year.

There is only one situation in which the MCAT should be repeated. This is if you have scored poorly in science and are positive your score was a fluke or know that you can do better. If you were sick on the day of the exam, misunderstood directions, or simply had other things on your mind and were distracted, then by all means repeat the MCAT. But if you have no good excuse for your performance and do not intend to do intensive remedial work, remember that two mediocre scores look worse than one.

The New MCAT is a tough exam by anybody's standards. You must do well on the test or your chances of acceptance are very slim. It is better to take the exam very seriously and to prepare for it than be angry with yourself after having done poorly. Everyone must take the New MCAT. The more confident you are, the better you will do. That confidence comes from good study habits and a well-planned review procedure prior to the test. Don't forget to order the *New MCAT Student Manual* from AAMC—it has some sample questions that you may want to look at.

CHAPTER 4

Applying to a Medical School—When, Where, and How

We have finally arrived at the really big step. So far all your energies have gone into fulfilling the requirements for medical school acceptance. You have completed most, if not all, of your premedical courses, taken the New MCAT, and amassed a portfolio of recommendations from professors. Now it is time to put those grades, test scores, and plaudits to use, and to couple them with some hard-core facts. Getting into a medical school is often a matter of having information other people do not have because they never bothered to find out and were never told. In this game, a little knowledge is an essential asset.

How many applications?

Let us begin our discussion with the surprising statistic that every year some medical school applicants apply to only one school. Can anyone afford to do that? Absolutely not! Not even if your father sits on the admissions committee and you are a *summa cum* from Harvard. If you are rejected by your one school, you are out of luck, whereas other students—with lesser credentials—who applied to numerous schools may have been accepted by one of them. One acceptance is really all it takes. Going to your last-choice school is infinitely preferable to going to none at all!

For the 1987–88 applicant pool the average applicant filed 9.5 applications for admission. There was a total of 266,900 applications by 28,123 persons. In recent years the number of applicants and the total number of applications filed have fluctuated, but the average number of applications per individual applicant has remained about the same—9.

This application spree had three causes: first, the stiff competition for medical school places; second, the growth of U.S. medical schools (this included new schools and the expansion of freshman class size in the majority of the existing schools); third, the American Medical College Application Service (AMCAS), which made it possible for the premedical student to apply to many schools while filing only one form. For the 1987–88 entering class, AMCAS processed over 25,600 applications, with more than 91% of all applicants applying to at least one AMCAS-participating school. For the 1987–88 entering class, 107 medical schools participated in AMCAS.

A study of medical school applicants, which appeared in the *Journal of Medical Education*, showed that, although the largest number of individuals applied to two to five schools, the acceptance rate was greatest for those applying to 26 to 30. The lowest acceptance rate was, predictably, for those who applied to two to five schools.

The first law of survival is to apply to as many schools as is feasible.

By feasible I do not mean that the number of applications you send out should be limited by your finances or by your boredom with filling out forms. You should apply to all schools to which your acceptance is a realistic possibility. No matter who you are, where you live, or what undergraduate college you attended, the number of such schools approaches ten or more.

There are a few rules of thumb to observe when choosing the schools to which to apply. First, it is always advisable to apply to schools in your part of the country, especially in your home state. State-supported medical schools are obliged to accept qualified in-state residents and usually consider only exemplary out-of-state students. An increasing number of private institutions are also heavily state-supported and lean towards taking in-state residents. Very few schools, in fact, are truly representative of the entire country. To my knowledge, few accept more applicants from any state other than their own, and none accepts more out-of-region than in-region enrollees.

Consider the schools in your own area as primary targets. Apply out of state only to those private institutions that profess to be geographically egalitarian. Pay particular attention to the fact that a few schools have an openly stated race preference.

*Forget about being the token white
at Howard.*

Above all, apply early.

Early decision

With reference to early application, some students may wish to participate in the Early Decision Plan (EDP). With this program, students apply to a single medical school in the spring of their junior year and await, hopefully, an acceptance by the next fall.

The EDP has two advantages. For the successful student it means the heat will be off by the beginning of the senior year. To the medical schools it represents a saving of both time and paperwork, since EDP students would otherwise have applied to an average of seven medical schools each, and, as most EDP candidates are highly qualified, their applications would have been processed in detail.

On the other hand, there are several limitations to the EDP program. The first is that, if accepted by the school applied to, the student is obliged to go there and may not apply elsewhere. The big disadvantage, however, is that the applicant is not certain of admission until October 1 of the senior year and may not apply to any other schools before that date. Thus, the rejected EDP applicant will be applying late to other schools.

The experience of the 77 medical schools using the Early Decision Plan in selecting their 1987–88 entering classes revealed that 806 applicants were accepted under this plan, or 52% of the total EDP candidates. Although not all medical schools participate in the EDP, I would advise my readers to apply to those that do. One reason is that medical school admissions today are *so* competitive that few students who are eventually accepted enjoy the privilege of selecting among schools. Most receive only one acceptance. Unless the October 1 acceptance date is moved up, it is true that you may have to apply late to other medical schools if rejected by your EDP school. However, this is more an inconvenience than a factor determining your possible future acceptance. Remember also that your big advantage on the EDP is having fewer applicants per place when you apply.

Cost of applying

Beg or borrow the money you will need to apply to medical schools. Application fees range from nothing to $10 or $50 at some places. It is possible to spend upwards of $500 filing applications, but if you have picked your schools carefully enough it is well worth the coin. Let's face it— you have already spent $25,000 to $50,000 for college alone. Should you be admitted, medical school will cost another $50,000 to $100,000. Application fees are a drop in the bucket.

I do not mean to suggest that you should apply to 100

medical schools or even 50 of them. Medical schools like to know that you want them as much as they want you. If you have made application to too many schools, your contention that you really want to go to one of them will seem hollow. However, if you have applied to a reasonable number of carefully selected schools, you can safely expound at your personal interview your reasons for wishing to attend each of them without your word being doubted. It will not appear that you want to go to any medical school that will accept you.

At your personal interviews, you may be asked to how many other schools you have applied. Being less than truthful will get you into a great deal of trouble, because all your applications are known to the AAMC. This is another reason to choose carefully.

Meeting the costs

Financial aid remains a major problem for most minority students. Middle-class youth may not give the cost of a medical education a second thought when applying for admission to medical college, but it must be borne in mind that 80% of all minority students in medical school come from families with incomes of less than $10,000 per year, and for 65%, the family income level is less than $5,000 yearly. The families of 20% of these students earn less than $3,000 a year.

Many organizations are helping minority students with funding, and the following is just a partial list of loans and fellowships available to minority students entering medicine:

"Make application to a reasonable number of carefully selected schools."

1. American Medical Women's Association, Inc., 465 Grand Street, New York, New York 10002. Minimum renewable loan programs are available. Applicants must be women students enrolled in their second, third, or fourth year at an accredited U.S. medical or osteopathic school. Repayment of loans begins one year after graduation.

2. Educational and Scientific Trust of the Pennsylvania Medical Society, 20 Erford Road, Lemoyne, Pennsylvania 17043. State residents with established financial need are eligible for loans at 6% interest.

3. Armed Forces Health Professions Scholarship Program: U.S. Air Force Recruiting Service, Medical Recruiting Division, Randolph AFB, Texas 78148. Scholarship recipients, who must agree to serve on active duty, are awarded tuition, associated educational costs, a stipend, and annual pay allowances of about $7,350.

4. National Medical Fellowships, Inc., 250 West 57th Street, New York, New York 10019. Fellowships, based primarily on financial need, are given on a competitive basis to minority students already accepted into medical school. They are renewable and cover tuition and living expenses.

5. National Health Service Corps Scholarship Program: Bureau of Health Personnel Development and Service, Room G-15, Center Building, 3700 East-West Highway, Hyattsville, Maryland 20782. Scholarship recipients, who must agree to serve in federally designated health manpower shortage areas, are awarded tuition, associated educational costs, and a monthly stipend.

In addition to the sources just listed, financial assistance is usually made available to medical students in the form of a mix between direct scholarships and loans. The amount of a scholarship award is determined by most schools primarily on the basis of economic need and not on academic performance. Thus, the student with a greater need and adequate to above-average academic record usually receives more scholarship assistance than loan money. Funds for either of these two types of assistance come from a variety of sources. Some are:

1. Directly from the medical school itself, usually from endowments made to the school for use in the support of students.

2. The federally supported Health Professions Student Loan Program, which provides funding to schools to be used for loans to students. A student may borrow up to a maximum of tuition plus $2,500 for each school year, repayable over a 10-year period with 9% interest.

3. The federally supported Guaranteed Student Loan Program (Federal Insured Student Loan Program) under which the student borrows money from a commercial bank, and the federal government guarantees the interest on the loan while the student goes to school. The student may borrow up to $5,000 per academic year, with a maximum total of $25,000. Repayment of the loan begins six months after graduation at 9% interest.

4. The federally supported National Direct Student Loan Program under which the student may borrow up to $12,000. The loan is repayable at 5% interest over a 10-year period, beginning 6 months after the student graduates.

5. The federally supported Health Education Assistance Loan Program, which provides insured loans of up to $20,000 a year. The loans are repayable over a 10- to

25-year period, beginning 9 to 12 months after training is completed.

6. The federal Scholarship Program for First-Year Students of Exceptional Financial Need, which provides tuition and a stipend, with no service payback requirement.

Minority students

Given equal qualifications, it has always been easier for certain groups of students to get into medical school than for others. In an effort to equalize the existing situation somewhat, medical schools are now bending over backwards to find qualified black, Puerto Rican, Asian, American Indian, Chicano, and women students. Much of this effort has been spurred by legal pressure on both state and federal levels.

In 1987–88, the nation's medical schools enrolled 1,441 underrepresented minority group students in their first-year classes—about 9% of the total first-year enrollment and three times the number that started medical school in 1960. These figures exclude Asians and Pacific Islanders.

AAMC figures for 1987–88 show that 6.2% of first-year medical students were black. Of these 994 students, 249 were attending either Howard University, Meharry Medical College, or Morehouse College, predominantly black institutions. The remaining students comprised an overall black enrollment of 4.6%.

Both first-year and total enrollments in medical school not only of black students, but also of American Indians, Mexican Americans, American Orientals, and mainland Puerto Ricans, have increased substantially since 1969. In the past ten years, the number of minority group applicants has fluctuated slightly each year, while the percentage of acceptances has also fluctuated, but in general has increased. In 1987–88, minority groups represented more than 8.8% of all students.

However, an acute nationwide shortage of black doctors was a major concern of the Annual Midwestern Conference sponsored by the National Medical Association (NMA)

"Medical schools are bending over backwards to solicit qualified minority group students."

recently. The 6,000 blacks out of 366,000 physicians in the United States represent only 2% as opposed to 11.7% of blacks in the total population.

Although the number of black students admitted to medical schools has been increasing in recent years, Alfred Fisher, the NMA'S Executive Director, considers that the pool of 700,000 blacks in higher education today could provide many more needed physicians. Because of hostility, competition, and other special problems black students face, he advocates a massive effort at the high school or early college level to prepare black medical aspirants. Native intelligence or talent is not enough, he warned. "When you consider that in the established white institutions there may be a hostile climate," he added, "it becomes very important for the individual student to be able to function academically and at the same time deal with the negative sociodynamics presented by the school itself." He stressed the difference that exists in undergraduate and professional school education for white and black alike, and the consequent need for early preparation.

Are quotas legal?

There have been questions whether the special efforts to recruit minority group students are appropriate, moral, and legal. Medical school administrators are beset from two sides. On the one hand, the angry white, middle-class applicant who has been rejected threatens to sue because an academically less well-qualified minority group student was accepted in his or her stead. On the other hand, there is an urgent national need for a more representative pool of physicians, and medical schools are well aware of that fact.

The expert opinion of five New York State Supreme Court justices was solicited by the AAMC several years ago. The consensus was that medical schools should be encouraged to increase minority enrollment and should undertake to insure appropriate support mechanisms. The following items were put forth by the judges for consideration:

1. The United States Supreme Court through various interpretations of the Constitution has not forbidden programs designed to increase access of minority groups to higher education. Measures instituted to correct racial imbalance have been upheld as constitutional.

2. Remedial and tutorial support programs in graduate and professional education are justified, necessary, and compelling.

3. Admissions committees should consider many factors in making a decision, and factors which go beyond statistical and mathematical determinants are allowable and important. A committee which goes beyond consideration of scores, grades, and rank order in aptitude tests seems eminently rational since it seeks to "humanize" the process of selecting prospective members of the profession.

4. Experimentation in selecting a class is both desirable and permitted. The tendency to get away from rigid categories is also healthy as long as experimental and special programs are published and clearly defined as different from the normal or traditional practices.

5. Admissions committees clearly have the obligation and right to expand or restrict admissions criteria—al-

though expansion of criteria is preferable and desirable. New and reasonable criteria may be included when considering applicants: that is, the nature of societal and community needs viewed from a national as well as a local perspective, the school's surrounding neighborhood and its special requirements, a clear preference on the part of the candidate to pursue a specific community-oriented experience upon completion of the course of study, and the applicant's extracurricular activities when examined against the immediate societal need and his or her long-range plan. No commitments by the student are necessary— just as an expression of future interest and an honest belief that the applicant will most probably fulfill the commitment which made that candidate's selection so compelling.

All of these factors and others provide a rational basis for making a judgment other than on a score or grade comparison. Grades alone cannot accurately predict performance.

6. Establishing given percentages or quotas of minority students to be accepted in a class poses predictable problems. This should be avoided at all costs.

7. Medical schools may stimulate interest by creating mechanisms for recruitment, tutorial support, and special preparatory courses in order to qualify and ultimately enroll minority students. [1]

Both *Medical Dimensions* and the *New Physician* have carried articles dealing with this complex problem. In May 1977, the *New Physician* ran a cover story about medicine's invisible practitioner—the minority physician. According to that study, given the stress of being a stranger in a strange world, it may not be surprising that, while the number of minorities applying to white schools has leveled off, the number of minority applicants to Howard and Meharry has multiplied. The opening of another predominantly black medical school at Morehouse also has perked minority interest.

It should be pointed out, however, that according to a June 1977 article in *Medical Dimensions*, when predominantly white schools began to admit minority students, they did so not by taking away admissions opportunities from white applicants, but by increasing the class size. For several years after the affirmative action push began, the absolute number of white students attending medical school increased. This is no longer true. The number of first-year black medical students increased by 68 from 1980 to 1981, but the number of white students declined.

In 1978 the Supreme Court handed down a landmark ruling on the famous Bakke case. Allan Bakke is a white engineer who brought a suit against the University of California Medical School at Davis. He charged that, because of a racial quota set by the school, he was twice rejected and was denied the right to compete for the reserved places. The Supreme Court ruled that racial quotas were illegal but that the factor of racial and ethnic origins could be used in the admissions process. Although quotas were disallowed, the affirmative action program by the universities was upheld.

Staying in can be harder than getting in

It would be unfair to minority group members who read this book not to present a complete picture of the situation. Although it may now be relatively easier than in the past for people from minority groups to get into medical school, graduating from one may prove difficult indeed. The fact is that the attrition rate among minority students is alarmingly high. Although the admissions committee may make concessions when evaluating a particular student's background, once in medical school that student is required to compete on exactly the same level as every other member of the class. Pledges of academic assistance may or may not be honored by the faculty, especially since many medical school professors may not look with particular favor on increased minority group enrollment. The student may be left by the wayside caught in a tangle of circumstances which may not only result in eventual academic failure but will also leave behind an overwhelming sense of personal failure.

To supply further insights into the nature of the problems many minority group members, especially blacks, face in medical school, I am excerpting an article which appeared in the January 1974 edition of *Medical Dimensions*. Although dated, it is still pertinent. It was written by the director of the minority student program at a midwestern medical school. He is an assistant dean and also sits on the admissions committee. To maintain his own future effectiveness in these posts, the article is anonymous. Dr. X, as he calls himself, considers his opinions representative of those of the medical profession in general.

Medical schools are doing a grave disservice to many of their minority students who, having been accepted after coercion from pressure groups and government agencies, lack the proper training to cope with the rigors of medical education. That disservice affects the society as well, for with every medical professor who sympathetically turns his back on low exam scores—passing students on their skin color and not performance—more inferior doctors are graduated with the power over life and death.

We are talking about minority students in general, but most of those students are in fact black. At a time when for every ten minority students admitted to school, only three will finish with a minimum of help, black organizations are pressuring medical schools to enroll more and more minority students. Four or more of those ten may graduate because of that same pressure, and at least three will fail. Yet at the Association of American Medical Colleges (AAMC) national convention the year before last in Miami, black pressure groups demanded a 24% minority enrollment nationwide. Is it realistic to expect that that many blacks can make it?

Dr. X goes on to summarize the academic career of a hypothetical inner city black student. He details the history of poor schools, environmental pressures, peer pressures which encourage violence rather than academics, parental neglect. But the student is dedicated to the idea of becoming a physician, so he gets a college scholarship. At college, he works very diligently, but his early lack of good training in the basics of study works against him. He gets good grades in some courses out of sympathy for his hard work. His MCAT scores are low, but he is admitted to medical school because of the sympathy "B" he got in chemistry. In medical school, he cannot compete and becomes part of the 30% to 40% of minority medical students who fail.

Dr. X analyzes the failure as the result of the student's background. As a high school student, he was too busy worrying about how to survive to have time to learn study skills, and while the black student in medical college was "stunned by the 'white man's school' and felt as though a mountain of information were falling on him in the first year, the white student, in his native environment, employed every one of his acquired skills with the stamina and hypertension he had been storing for the task." Psychologically, the black student is unable to withstand the pressures of medical school, and Dr. X is convinced that no matter how hard a medical school wants to try, "it will never be able to make an eager young track star run a four-minute mile while wearing lead boots."

The solution, Dr. X feels, is one which unfortunately will do currently aspiring minority students little good: "The preparation a minority student needs for medical school should take place long before he graduates from college. Study skills should be taught in grammar school, not in medical school. The drive necessary to turn thousands of facts into the practice of medicine should be acquired long before the postgraduate levels."

Medical school *is* an incredible head-trip—especially for the poorly prepared. For this reason, it is *imperative* that minority students be certain of the medical school's commitment to them, in terms of tutorial help and financial aid, before accepting a place in the freshman class. There is a whole world of difference between an attitude that says, "We accepted you, now show us how good you are" and "We accepted you because we want you to become a physician, and we will help you because we have an investment in your future."

Women students—another minority

The new pressure on medical schools to increase minority enrollment has also affected a woman applicant's chances of being accepted, but this does not mean that admissions committees may not still show a reluctance to accept women. The question foremost in their minds when considering a woman applicant is, How will she use her medical education after she receives it? In the past, women medical students had a higher attrition rate than men. Fearing they would be unable to mix marriage and a career, they usually abandoned the latter. Admissions committees also fear that even after having completed medical school many women may soon leave the profession to have and raise children. Although such trends are changing rapidly, it takes time for the news to reach those admissions committee members whose ideas about women in the professions are, shall we say, traditional.

"Woman has so apparent a function in certain medical specialties and seemingly so assured a place in general medicine under some obvious limitations that the struggle for wider educational opportunities for the sex was pre-destined to an early success in medicine." That was written by Abraham Flexner in the famous *Flexner Report* of 1910. However, although women were freely admitted to medical college in those days, only a small percentage of those who matriculated eventually graduated.

Flexner's conclusion was that "as the opportunities of women have increased, not decreased . . . their enroll-ment should have augmented, if there is any strong demand for women physicians or any strong ungratified desire on the part of women to enter the profession, one or the other of these conditions is lacking—perhaps both."

Had Mr. Flexner interviewed some of those women he might have discovered other reasons why only 15% to 20% of the matriculants graduated from medical school in 1909–1910. Family commitments, social pressures, and economics were doubtless on the list of reasons a woman had for leaving medical school before graduation. These pressures are still effective, but today most women who enter medical school not only graduate but also outperform the men.

A woman called to a medical school for an interview should anticipate being asked how she plans to mix a marriage and a career. The committee will make the tacit assumption that if the woman is not now married, she eventually will be. However, they do not hold firmly to the idea that marriage and a career are incompatible for a woman, so there's no reason to say you're going to be a missionary doctor when you really do hope to marry and raise a family.

Statistics show that the percentage of women enrolled in medical school is increasing every year, although these figures are also affected by the recent overall decline in applicants. In competition for the available places, the 1987–88 applicant pool included 10,411 women, 59.6% of whom were accepted. Women accounted for 37% of the applicant pool for that year and 36.2% of new first-year entrants. It is the opinion of most medical school admissions officials that by the 1990s women will constitute upwards of 40% of the enrolled medical students in the country. Much of this increase in women enrollees has been among minority group students.

An interesting statistic is that only 1.9% of the women who were accepted in 1971 failed to matriculate. This number has been steadily declining since 1968 when 10.2% of those accepted failed to enroll. Clearly, more women than ever before feel that they wish to pursue a medical career, and although I cannot find any statistics to support my surmise, I suspect that the attrition rate of women medical students has also been declining in the past ten years. In my own medical school class of 105, eight women began the program in 1969 and none failed to graduate. Of the eight, three graduated in the top 10% of the class and were elected to Alpha Omega Alpha, the medical honor society.

The number and the percentage of women in residency programs have also been increasing steadily. As recently as 1977, one third of all specialties had no female residents. Today, women are represented in all specialty and subspecialty areas and constitute 28% of all postgraduate trainees.

Special interest groups

Many people still believe that there are special interest groups influential in getting students into a medical school. Thus Alumni Associations take on an undue importance, as does the private individual who makes a substantial contribution to the medical school library. Rarely does it happen any more that anyone gets into a medical school simply because a close relative went there and, contrary to the mythology, nobody buys his or her way into a medical school today. It just isn't done. There is that occasional student who, by directive of the dean, must be admitted, but this is by no means a common occurrence. Indeed, sons and daughters of faculty members gain admission no more easily than anyone else.

Given personal idiosyncrasies and individual preferences, it may safely be said that medical school admissions committees are about as democratic a group as you will find anywhere.

Making application—the AMCAS

Filling out application forms can be tedious work, not to mention complex, costly, and likely to produce considerable anxiety. To make things somewhat easier the AAMC has devised the American Medical College Application Service (AMCAS), a centralized process by which the student fills out only one application for admission, furnishes only one set of transcripts, and applies to as many of the participating medical schools as desired. The medical school then notifies the applicant of further steps necessary to complete the application at each particular school. The service's big advantage to the applicant is that it saves time and paperwork. It serves the medical schools by transmitting only completed application forms standardized by computer and by providing statistical analyses. The student must still pay each school's application fee plus an AMCAS service fee which is determined by the number of applications sent out.

You must request the services of AMCAS by submitting a completed "Application Request" for the specific year of your projected medical school entrance. The request blanks vary from year to year, so make sure you have the correct one. (Early summer is the best time to complete the forms.) Complete the form as carefully and accurately as possible and xerox a copy of the filled-out pages for your files. Then submit the forms and appropriate service fees directly to AMCAS.

The transcripts

The next step is to request the registrars of *all* the colleges you've attended to mail official transcripts to AMCAS. Expect from AMCAS an "Acknowledgement of Receipt" noting all received and outstanding material. A "Transmittal Notification" will follow from AMCAS when all material has been received, processed, and forwarded to your designated schools. Finally, anticipate requests from individual schools for your letters of recommendation.

The AMCAS form requires much objective information. Needless to say, you should fill out these parts accurately, since a mistake here will delay the processing and forwarding of your transcript at least two weeks. A few questions give you the opportunity to reply in a short paragraph, and the form also provides a page for personal comments which may be used in any way you wish. If there is anything about you that makes you an extraordinary or unusual applicant, it should be mentioned here. Students, I have noticed, tend to minimize their non-academic achievements. The fact that you may have played in a symphony orchestra, were a collegiate athlete or held a political office is relevant and worth stating. So is your involvement in school clubs and organizations if they were anything more than merely social. Summer work experience is also important, especially if you worked in an allied health field.

A friend of mine was once employed as a hospital orderly, but neglected to say so on his medical school applications. He thought that all premeds had done some hospital work and that being a mere orderly (rather than a research assistant) was not worth mentioning. Actually, most premedical students do not have any hospital ex-

perience before going to medical school. Even if you were
an ambulance driver, aide, or simply a volunteer, make
certain you note it. Far from looking demeaning, it will
show the admissions committee that you had the initiative
to work in a medical environment before making a final
decision on a medical career. For some of you it might
even have been the impetus to choose medicine as your
vocation—if so, say so. Also, a person who has worked in
a hospital setting has a much easier time answering the
perennial question asked at the personal interviews: "Why
do you want to become a physician?"

Having done hospital work is clearly advantageous.
More than anything else, it helps you make up your own
mind about choosing medicine. Other service-oriented
work is just as important, for it shows your interest in and
compassion for other people. Have you worked as a
counselor in a camp for emotionally disturbed children,
cardiacs, or diabetics? Were you an adviser in government-
supported projects like Head Start or Upward Bound?
Did you work in a day-care center or free clinic? Have
you taught children or adults to do crafts? Did you do
social work in a family center? Drug counseling? Tutoring?
Take care of a sick grandmother? Say so!

What makes you different?

Medical schools are also impressed by work which,
although not dealing directly with other people, involved
the completion of a task. Thus, editing your school
newspaper or literary magazine, researching, writing and
publishing a paper, or being a fine artist are all relevant
to your application. Indeed, anything about you that
makes you different from most everyone else is precisely

what *is* relevant. If you are a top basketball star, a golfer, a tournament chess player, airplane pilot, or writer, you must say so. Medical schools look for diversity in their freshman class. It is not hard to find students with high GPAs and MCATs —they are plentiful. It is hard to find students who bring unusual backgrounds to the study of medicine.

Virtually every application has a page for personal comments. Some ask that you write about why you want to become a doctor while others let you do with the space as you wish. In all cases the page should be used and under no circumstances should it be returned blank. If you are coming to medicine late in your college career or after you have been out of school, then you have some explaining to do and you should start here. If your father is a nonprofessional (farmer, laborer, etc.) the admissions committee will want to know when and why you decided to study medicine. You can use this space to tell them.

If you are a woman or from a minority group, you might want to talk about how this has influenced your decision. And if you are, like most applicants, a white middle-class male, you can use the space to list your reasons for choosing medicine for your life's work.

Dr. Woodrow W. Morris, Associate Dean of the University of Iowa College of Medicine, made these comments about the personal comments page on application forms in a recent issue of *The Advisor:*

"The way in which applicants use this blank space has already proved useful to admissions committees in the realm of affording them a little insight into the personality make-up of the writer. And some of the ways the space has been used have been wonderful to behold. Among these are: straightforward appeals for admission, autobio-

*Anything about you that makes you different from
most everyone else is precisely what is relevant.*

graphical sketches, philosophical dissertations on everything from the state of mankind in the 1970's to the essential qualities of the complete physician. Other uses have included doggerel verse such as the student who apparently wanted to impress the reader with his knowledge of anatomy by writing:

> The cow is of the bovine ilk,
> One end is moo,
> The other milk.

Still others have filled the space with more ambitious creative poetry, again on the various kinds of topics listed above. Perhaps the most unusual of all have been those creations produced by applicants with an artistic flair—everything from chiaroscuro productions to caricatures. Finally, it should be noted that there are occasionally those brave souls who dare look at the blank space, and leave its pristine surface alone. (This, it should be observed, often leaves admissions committees in doubt as to whether the student did not wish to reveal his [*sic*] or her self, or whether the applicant simply had nothing to say.)

It would be a service to both applicants and admissions committees if preprofessional advisers would encourage their students to make optimum use of the opportunity provided to them for expressing their individual thoughts and talents. Similarly, it would be helpful if future AMCAS materials provided both more space for 'personal comments' and more detailed instructions concerning the use of this important space."

The essay should be typewritten and grammatically correct, at the very least. A great deal of care should be taken in organizing it. A good idea is to write a rough draft, put it away, and pull it out a few days later, and see how it looks to you. In the meantime you might think of things you wish to add or delete, or you might consider a different focus to give the essay. This little essay is far more important than any paper you will write in college, so judge the time you spend on it accordingly. Given the fact that many incoming medical students cannot even write a coherent paragraph, a well-written essay is downright impressive.

Recommendations

After MCAT scores and your GPA, recommendations are the most important criterion for admission to a medical school, even more important than the personal interview. Many students tend to discount the significance of recommendations by erroneously assuming them all to be complimentary. It is true that most recommendations are positive in their appraisal of a student, but some are more positive than others, and some are just negative enough to keep you out of medical school.

In the past, the usual way of obtaining recommendations was to go directly to individual professors and have them fill out and submit forms from the medical school. Three recommendations usually sufficed, at least one of which was to come from a teacher in the premedical sciences. Today, that process has become much more sophisticated, with most colleges having premedical advisory committees which collate recommendations from all of your college professors and write a composite letter to the medical schools. At my university, premeds were required to have all of their instructors fill out a mimeographed form and file it with the premedical committee. After four years of college a student would have accumulated forty-odd appraisals from which the committee could then begin to draft a letter of recommendation.

The option of handpicking the professors whom you wish to ask for an evaluation is becoming much less common, but it still exists at schools without premedical committees. The student should beware, however, since some professors with whom you may be on a good footing socially may not be able to vouch for your academic ability, laboratory competence, or good character. It is not unreasonable to ask a professor if he or she is able to write you a good recommendation before asking for one.

The premedical student might also want to make the faculty member whose recommendation is being solicited aware of the kind of letters medical schools like to receive—namely, letters that reflect real knowledge of the student and his or her past performance. Comments which help put the student's performance in perspective and make clear the letter writer's opportunity to evaluate the student are very helpful. A comment such as, "He is one of the best premedical students I have had in this laboratory class for some time," or "She ranked in the upper one-third of this seminar for laboratory students," help the medical schools interpret the comments made on the student. If the class is one for majors or has special qualifications for enrollment, it should be noted. The basis for evaluation—e.g., two midterm examinations and a final test, or two three-hour laboratory sessions a week throughout the quarter—helps the medical school interpret the evaluation.

Medical school admissions committees tend to think in terms of rank categories. For example, if you received an honor, they would be delighted to know just how selective an honor it was. If you were "highly recommended" by the premedical committee, what percentage of all the premeds were similarly recommended? Being elected to Phi Beta Kappa as a physics major may be more significant than gaining the same honor as a humanities student if, at your institution, it is rare for physics students to be elected. Or if, for example, you have received a highly competitive summer research fellowship, you may ask your professor to comment on the conditions of the competition. If, on the other hand, you were the only applicant for the position, the less said the better.

The student should attempt to solicit a recommendation from the faculty member with the highest professorial rank. An outstanding recommendation from a full professor is much more impressive than one from a laboratory instructor, and it carries far more weight.

Some students simply have had no personal contact with their teachers and have difficulty obtaining recommendations. Medical school admissions committees feel that it is the student's responsibility to get to know professors, especially the faculty adviser. The reason for this is that student-teacher contact is an integral part of college education, and the good student will make an effort to establish it—even if only for the sake of getting a recommendation. Medical schools do not frown on aggressive students!

Not only are they absurdly flattering, but there is rarely any pertinent character analysis. These recommendations have nothing whatever to do with your ability to perform in medical school or to be a physician.

Certain types of recommendations, however, may be helpful. If, for instance, you have worked in a research

Recommendations from people outside the academic sphere—the family minister, priest, or rabbi, relatives, or friends—are usually uniformly laudatory and should be avoided.

lab during your summer vacations, you might ask the director to write a recommendation for you, especially if he or she was favorably impressed with your work. A letter from any physician or hospital administrator under whom you have worked in a nonacademic setting can be of use. In fact, anyone who has known you in a professional context should be considered as a source of letters of recommendation. They may be mailed to your school's premedical advisory committee or sent directly to the medical schools to which you have applied.

The importance of the recommendation is not to reaffirm your academic competence; your grades and MCAT already attest to that. Rather, recommendations serve basically to assess your character and to explain any discrepancies that may exist on your academic record. If you are a more capable student than your transcript indicates, perhaps your recommendations will state this. If your grades dropped sharply one semester because you held a part-time job to earn enough money to continue in school, your recommendations should make this clear.

On the other hand, if you are an antisocial dolt with no personality, your recommendations are likely to say so, and they will be a severe handicap to your getting into a medical school.

One problem connected with recommendations concerns the confidentiality of the evaluations. There is the real possibility that, in the near future, files will be "open" and all students will have access to them. Premedical students will then have the option of examining their evaluations and either removing unfavorable letters or at least answering them.

Already the confidentiality of files has become a legal issue in several states. Should files become "open" and accessible, it follows that either premedical evaluations will become testimonials or professors will simply refuse to write them. Obviously, faculty members will write different letters if they know their letters are going to be read by the student than if these comments can remain confidential. All this will be to the disadvantage of superior students, since mediocre students will pull those letters they do not want sent out. The result, in all probability, will be more reliance on word of mouth (usually a phone call) for such information and less on letters of recommendation.

The interview

The personal interview is usually rated fourth in importance for medical school admission—behind GPA, MCAT, and recommendations. Indeed, for the highly qualified student the personal interview is a mere formality, done to assure the admissions committee that the candidate is capable of responding in a situation of stress such as the interview. It also affords the candidate an opportunity to see the medical school and ask whatever questions are considered pertinent. Not every medical school requests an interview. Some think they are irrelevant and others have found them too subjective to be a worthwhile method of assessing a student's future performance.

On the average, medical schools today interview approximately 15% to 20% of the total number of applicants. If a prestigious eastern medical school receives 5,000 applications or more, the admissions committee will probably interview almost 1,000 people. Thus, even at the interview stage, you still must convince the committee of your desire to attend their particular school of medicine. In other words, being granted an interview is great, but your job isn't over yet.

It was pointed out at one recent medical conference dealing with admissions interviewing that too many applicants fail to realize one very important factor—physicians, by nature of their training, are professional interviewers. Doctors are experts at "fishing out" information from people even if these people resist initial attempts at probing. Doctors are trained to interview patients and to look for signs that a patient is holding back information or harboring false ideas about his or her individual condition. If you are unsure of yourself or unconvincing as a future doctor, then the interviewing physician will easily spot this and take note.

Actually, the interview is a humanizing aspect of the medical school admissions process. This is your chance to sell the product you know best—yourself. The interview gives you the opportunity to see the particular school and to meet some faculty members and students. Take advantage of the situation and explore the school, ask questions, and try to form an impression of the school in your own mind. The interview is a mutual exchange; make it work for you.

The interviews are established to explore several different areas of the applicants' backgrounds. They test the motivation, preparation, commitment and sincerity of the applicant. Believe it or not, these seemingly intangible factors can be easily assessed. Motivation we have discussed before in terms of summer work and understanding the role of the physician in our society. Preparation is another important aspect of any application. The interviewers will want to know if you took the proper science courses at your college or if you substituted "physics for poets" for the required course. How well did you perform on the MCAT and did you take it seriously enough to prepare for it in advance? What is your level of commitment to medicine as demonstrated by your knowledge of the different types of specialties and practices? Do you follow newspaper articles about medical issues or is your only desire in life an MD license plate? Lastly, has your sincere desire to become a physician been rooted in your own desires and intellect or are you a last-minute convert to the medical mode? How seriously have you considered the alternative health careers and why did you choose medicine as opposed to social work?

Being able to answer these questions for yourself is the primary goal here. You have to be honest with yourself before you can be honest with your probing interviewer. Don't have any stock or prepared answers ready for your interview—shoot from the hip and just be as honest as possible.

If you are lucky enough to be invited for a personal interview, you should certainly try to learn as much as possible about the school you are visiting. Don't go to the interview ignorant. By all means read the school brochure or catalogue beforehand. It is also a good idea to skim over your application to the school to refresh your strong points. Of course, this also means that you should copy everything before you mail your applications away. Think of the mail as a conspiracy against you and you'll see how easy it is to learn to copy everything first.

Never, never be late for an interview. If your train or plane is late then it is your responsibility to phone the school and explain the circumstances involved. This is a signal to the school of your maturity level and coolheadedness. Try to arrive early for your interview if possible. This way you will have some time to look around and start to relax a little. If your interviewer is late, do not make any reference to the amount of time you had to wait. Believe me, he or she was probably doing something more important at the moment than you. Don't worry, you were not forgotten.

Dress appropriately. Although this should be obvious to any college senior, you wouldn't believe what some people look like for an interview. Men don't have to look like an advertisement for Brooks Brothers, but certainly wear a suit if you can. If money is a problem, then a quiet sport coat and unobtrusive tie are in order. Avoid leisure suits and simple sweaters—they may go over well in certain parts of the country but aren't certainly going to help your case. If your medical school application picture was taken with your glasses on, then wear them to the interview; don't sit there squinting at the interviewer for the sake of vanity. Interviewers are not interested in filling a class with Robert Redford types.

For women, the rules are similar: Slack suits, no matter how appealing, should NOT be worn to a formal medical school interview. A simple skirt and blouse or pretty dress that is conservatively cut is far more appropriate. Avoid excessive makeup or fancy jewelry. You won't impress anyone with that kind of approach. Dress for the seriousness of the situation and you should come out looking just fine.

Probably the most important recommendation anyone can make is the necessity for being completely honest at an interview. If you don't know something, don't be afraid to say so. This will demonstrate your own level of self-confidence and bearing. If you have certain questions about the school's program, then voice them at the appropriate time. Be honest about your financial needs and be prepared to discuss them intelligently if the situation arises. Be prepared to discuss any deficiences in your record and try to avoid "buttering up" the interviewer at all costs. Do not second-guess the person questioning you and just try to be yourself. What you say and how you say it are what counts.

Definitely try to assert your positive aspects during the medical school interview. If you are particularly proud of a certain research project you completed, then say so in an effective manner without pontificating. Try to convey your own enthusiasm for a particular field to your interviewer. If you did poorly in one course because of a teacher conflict, then tactfully explain the situation without attacking the professor involved. Never berate your own school, as this is a sign of immaturity. Of course, it is also important to be a good listener as well as talker.

Keep your eyes on the person talking to you and pay attention.

Use your native tongue to your advantage and avoid the pitfalls of everyday usage. The interview is no place for *like* and *you know*. You don't have to sound like a walking thesaurus, but do avoid hackneyed expressions. Put your best foot forward and think before you speak. It is better to pause with silence than to say *um* twenty times in one conversation. Absolutely avoid impressing the interviewer with a small amount of medical talk you may know. This could be disastrous if he or she follows up this line of conversation and your knowledge runs out after two sentences.

Try to relax and be yourself. I realize that for some individuals, this will be the most difficult part of the interviewing process. If you really are excessively nervous, then state this fact. It may help to caution the interviewer to be a little more understanding about your anxiety. If you approach the interview with PMA (Positive Mental Attitude), then you will be much cooler and self-assured without being cocky. If you are the knee-trembling type, then try this simple, proven technique used by public speakers and politicians. When sitting facing the interviewer, simply curl your toes up as tight as you can, of course without grimacing or removing your shoes! The tension created by this simple maneuver will relax the rest of your body and the shakes will miraculously disappear. Practice this trick if you want when you go out on a first date and you'll see your nervousness vanish. Good public speakers are really a bundle of nerves inside, but outwardly they are the essence of cool. This little trick helps to relax you and make you more confident.

Lastly, remember to write down the names of the people who interviewed you. This serves two functions: It is always a good idea to send a brief thank-you card to an interviewer, stating the following:

Dear Dr.........,

Thank you for taking the time to discuss my application for the (Name of School) on (Date). I am looking forward to hearing from you soon.

Sincerely,

....

This will help to reinforce your name in the interviewer's mind and also demonstrate your "level of breeding." Good manners are *always* good policy. Secondly, if you have occasion to write to the school for more information or for another reason, don't hesitate to include your interviewer's name in the note or, even better, write directly to the admissions committee, care of that particular individual.

Questions most frequently asked at the medical school interview include those about your family background, school activities, summer employment, hobbies, what you do to relax, and how you handle school pressures. The other group deals mainly with standard, yet very important questions about your fields of possible interest, why medicine, and your thoughts on current issues such as abortion or euthanasia. Remember, the interviewer wants to see how you react under fire and he or she is not concerned with your own opinion, per se. Total truthfulness is the best approach for the interview confrontation.

There are certain circumstances when an interview can assume great importance. Sometimes committee members may be reluctant to accept a candidate because of special questions raised by his or her application. The only advice I can give in this case is to answer all questions at the interview and to be yourself. Remember that the ultimate question is always: "Who is this human being who will someday take care of other human beings?" Make the committee feel as good about you as you feel about yourself.

NOTES

1. M. S. Begun, "Legal Considerations Related to Minority Group Recruitment and Admissions," in *Journal of Medical Education,* Vol. 48, pp. 556–559.

CHAPTER 5

How Medical School Admissions Committees Evaluate Applicants

Since I have never been a member of a medical school admissions committee, my information in this chapter is admittedly secondhand. It is true that some schools do have students serving on this committee, but they are few. In most cases, admissions committee members are recruited from the medical school faculty to serve varying periods of time, usually from one to three or four years. The assistant or associate dean of student affairs is commonly a permanent member, while other members rotate, for the job is time consuming, and most faculty members have other obligations.

An admissions committee may have as few as five or as many as fifteen members, selected from all areas of the clinical and basic sciences. They will try to be fair, but, like most human beings, they see the ideal applicant as someone who is quite like themselves. Therefore the more members a committee has, the greater are your chances of finding an advocate.

Can the applicant make it?

Medical school admissions committees look for three things when they evaluate applicants. First they ask, can he or she get through the program? This is crucial. There are many who have the desire to become physicians, are congenial enough, and have perhaps the capacity for genuine concern and empathy for others. However, unless the committee feels that an applicant has made the commitment and can do the work, they will not recommend acceptance. Medical schools are acutely aware of the need for physicians and do not want to waste a precious place on an applicant who is not likely to complete the program. Second, admissions committee members are concerned about the character of the people who will one day practice on the public. They feel it is their job to select students who will not only become competent physicians but who are also reasonably stable and responsible. Finally, they ask whether it is fair to admit a specific applicant in preference to someone else, and while all members of admissions committees will admit to personal biases about what constitutes a desirable applicant, there is a universal attempt to be fair and impartial. To avoid pressure, members of the committee often remain anonymous.

With the enormous number of applicants to medical school each year it is not possible for every member of an admissions committee to review each application. The number of applications may vary from 160 to as many as

7,500 for anywhere from 25 to 250 places. Your application may be reviewed by one or several members of the committee, but certainly not by all of them.

The usual procedure is as follows: The admissions committee probably won't even consider your folder until all the numerical information is at hand. In other words, it is best to have your transcripts and MCAT scores sent to the schools as early as possible. Once all the information is assembled, your folder is completed and ready for review.

Many schools differ in their review process. Unfortunately, due to budget and personal constraints, many public medical colleges have resorted to a computerized check-off system for folders. All the numbers are fed into a computer formula, and if a certain cutoff point is reached, the applicant is invited for a personal interview. If the cutoff point of a specific GPA and MCAT combination is not attained, the applicant is summarily rejected.

At many other schools, the situation is not as grim. The folder is assembled and the GPA may not even be computed. The applicant may be invited for an interview based on the essay or personal comments section of the application. This is a very time-consuming process but in an important way is a reflection of the caliber of the schoool and its faculty's commitment to the students. Several schools utilize a two-stage process where the applicant is asked to first send his or her grades and MCATs and then, if satisfactory, to complete the essay portion of the application. Happily, more schools are turning to their own students for help in this area. Medical students may even serve as voting members of the admissions committee and have equal rights as full faculty members.

To review, cumulative grade point averages as well as grades obtained in science courses, scores on the MCAT, descriptions of extracurricular activities, letters of recommendation from faculty members and letters from past employers are evaluated. If the application is given a high rating by each of the people who did the screening, the applicant will most likely be invited for the prized personal interview. At least he or she will have cleared the first hurdle.

Determining the motivation

After a candidate clears initial screening, his or her whole application is carefully evaluated. Special attention is given to five areas. First, the admissions committee ascertains what courses went into producing the student's GPA. Required and science-related courses are noted, as well as those that show broadness of education. If there is a discrepancy between GPA and MCAT scores, a candidate's course work is looked at for a possible explanation. Basically, however, the admissions committee is interested in what turned the applicant on in college. The same can be said for extracurricular activities. However, good grades and no extracurricular activities may be indicative of a person who used up all available energy supplies just to do well academically. Students who list many extracurricular activities and have also done well in class are thought likely to be capable medical students.

Just as extracurricular activities provide the admissions committee with insight into the applicant as a human being, the personal statement also lets the student seem more of an individual. The personal statement details the applicant's motivation for seeking a medical career. The expressed attitude toward service takes a particularly high priority in the committee's evaluation. If you state a strong desire to work with people, but your transcript shows you took only science courses and your summer job was as a lab assistant, the committee will sense a discrepancy and will begin to doubt your suitability as a medical student. The committee must feel that society is going to profit when you become a physician, that your motives are service-oriented rather than self-aggrandizing.

Committee members are adept at judging such an amorphous concept as motivation. Ideally, they look for a certain group of characteristics in a potential physician. In an Ethics of Health Care study performed by the National Academy of Sciences, the top seven personal attributes used in the selection process were as follows: 1) humanitarian beliefs and sincerity, 2) evidence of psychological maturity, 3) initiative, perseverance and enthusiasm, 4) ability to communicate effectively, 5) interest and knowledge of medicine, 6) general intellectual interest and cultural development, and 7) imagination or creativity. Furthermore, in the same study, faculty members on the admissions committee of a particular school endorsed *alert, conscientious, enthusiastic,* and *honest* as the adjectives used to describe the best candidates they had seen or folders they had reviewed at one time.

According to Dr. Marvin Fogel of the Mount Sinai School of Medicine, "the verbal and action offerings apparent in your credentials will be the following: the undeniable fact of your desire for knowledge and its implementation against disease; your quite evident compassion for the ill and the solving of their problems; your positive ability to work with people even under vexing circumstances; your unequivocal understanding of the continuing, unceasing education process that the practicing physician must undergo; the inescapable sacrifice of outside interest time in order to devote yourself to the 'jealous lover,' which is the profession of medicine."

Lastly, another favorite guidepost, or indicator of a candidate's "motivation level," is the summer activities. Were the applicant's months away from school used to get a great tan, or did he or she attempt to learn more about the complex medical field? More on this appears in Chapter 7; be sure to see this information before planning your next beach-bum summer!

Family background is important in only two instances. The first is if the applicant's family is poor. This is usually taken as an indication of a highly motivated student who has had to fight all the way along the line. However, the committee may want to know why this candidate decided on medicine and what the choice means financially to the family. The second case is that of a physician's son or daughter who applies to medical school. The committee may become suspicious and want to be sure that the student's decision was not influenced by family pressure. The committee knows that attrition rates for the sons and daughters of MDs are higher than for the offspring of any other professional or nonprofessional group.

Letters of recommendation from undergraduate faculty members assume great importance in the committee's evaluation of an applicant. Not all recommendations are uniformly glowing. Some are merely perfunctory, while others may be ambiguous and need clarification and still others may be unfavorable. In these letters, admissions committees look for statements regarding the candidate's motivation or commitment to medicine, his or her integrity, originality, and dependability. Any inconsistencies

"It gives the interviewer a chance to see the candidate as a human being."

between GPA, personal statement, and faculty recommendations must be explained.

On the basis of the appraisal of the application, a student may be put into one of four categories:

1. Invited for interview—if satisfactory, accepted.

2. Invited for interview—use interview to clarify problems or inconsistencies in the record. Explain red flags. Give the student an opportunity to explain parts of the record that cause committee members some concern before acceptance is offered.

3. Hold category—hold until another group of applicants has been evaluated or until additional information is received, such as grades of courses in progress.

4. Rejected on the basis of the record.

If the candidate falls into either category one or two, he or she will be interviewed.

The interview itself serves two functions. It gives the interviewer a chance to see the candidate as an individual rather than a collection of papers in a file somewhere. Second, it enables the interviewer to clarify items in the application if that is necessary.

Being invited for a personal interview is an accomplishment in itself. Once invited, you can be assured that your folder will get a very thorough going-over. Beware, however, that an interview appointment does not mean automatic acceptance. Several hurdles lie ahead.

CHAPTER 6

Rejection and Your Alternatives

Rejection and reapplication

A favorite question posed at the end of medical school interviews is, "What will you do if you don't get into a medical school?" This is not usually asked out of any genuine concern for your future but to assess the strength of your conviction to pursue medicine. Don't say, "There's always teaching biology or selling encyclopedias."

The person who really wants to become a doctor will outline specific plans to wait, perhaps do some more course work, and reapply the next year. If again unsuccessful, a foreign medical school would be the next step. Or even more confidence can be shown and the student can say that all other alternatives are second-rate, no serious consideration had ever been given to being anything other than a physician, and he or she feels perfectly capable of completing the medical school curriculum.

This is an appropriate answer to the examiner's question

but is certainly not the most realistic way to think about the problem. In other countries, where medical school enrollment is open to all who have college degrees, the question of alternatives would be superfluous. Here, where demand for places in medical school far outstrips supply, the issue is crucial. To preserve your sanity, not to mention your livelihood, the issue of alternatives must be faced early in your premed career. To be sure, there are three possibilities for the rejected applicant: choose an alternative profession, reapply, or attend a foreign medical school. Although any combination of alternatives may be pursued simultaneously, it is necessary to plan for the first one well in advance of your graduation date.

To be able to select a suitable alternative career while still a premed, you must be very sure of your motives for wanting to enter medicine. This will also be an asset when, should you become a physician, it comes time to choose a field of specialization. Basically, you must have an accurate picture of *what* it is doctors actually do, and then ask yourself, *"Why* do I want to become a doctor?" The "what" problem can be taken care of by visiting medical centers and physicians' offices and observing what goes on. Work in a hospital for a summer. Read medical periodicals. Talk to physicians. Talk to patients. The "why" requires more insight, and you might avail yourself of help from a therapist in order to get it all straightened out.

Once you've got your head together, the question of alternative professions can be faced intelligently, should the need arise. If your motives for entering medicine are strictly materialistic, then for the amount of time invested, the business professions and dentistry yield much higher dividends. If the motivating force is status and prestige, law or politics is a suitable alternative. Anyone interested in basic medical research can pursue it almost as easily with a PhD as an MD. Altruistic motives will probably find gratification in the service professions—notably social work or psychology. The clinical aspects of medicine can be duplicated in nursing and in physician assistant programs, as well as by training in the alternative health fields such as acupuncture, chiropractic, massage, and nutrition counseling.

Consider reapplying

The issue of reapplication to medical school deserves some discussion. Clearly, it is more difficult to get into a medical school the second time around, although many students have entered by this route. These students most often have strong academic records and either applied to the wrong schools or sought admission in an especially competitive year. They are not marginal students. As a rule they are the students who are most surprised at being rejected. They fully expected to be admitted to a medical school, and their premedical advisers expected them to be as well. They are the students who can point to others with lesser credentials who were successful where they failed. For such students, reapplication is feasible. The questions are when to reapply and what to do in the meantime.

Reapply to any school that has encouraged you to do so and to any school where you were interviewed or put on a waiting list. If you initially applied to the "wrong" schools, as previously defined, find out what the "right" schools are for you and apply to all of them. Reapply early. The question of what to do in the interim has various answers. A school may urge that you take additional courses or enter a special program with the incentive that if you do well enough they will accept you, reconsider you, or something in between these extremes. The choice is yours. I would only suggest that the more positive the incentive the more you should consider following the recommendation.

Many students with bachelor's degrees enter graduate school for a year as a stepping-stone to medical school. There is a growing feeling in medical schools, however, not to accept candidates in the process of obtaining a higher degree until after that degree has been earned. Thus, entering a graduate school might result in a two- to three-year delay before acceptance by a medical college. In addition, you will once again be under the same pressure to perform academically as you were when an undergraduate. I would not recommend this route to the nonscience major and would advise it only for science majors who feel the extra science will be useful to them in their medical field.

Rejection by medical school requires a careful consideration of the applicant's weaknesses. Academic shortcomings can be remedied by repeating courses or taking extra ones as a special student. Low MCATs necessitate retaking that exam after extensive preparation. A student with a one-sided education stressing academics exclusively may find two years in the Peace Corps or performing other service-oriented jobs will prove an asset.

Reapplication to medical school is itself a testimonial to the applicant's persistence and desire to become a physician. Indeed, such students often graduate at the top of their medical school class. Before investing time in the reapplication process, an applicant must proceed from a realistic appraisal of the situation. With competition for medical school places becoming stiffer each year, it would be self-defeating for someone with a weak record to stay in the race. An objective evaluation of your chances for success should be solicited from the premedical adviser or other counselor. It is important for your own mental health to know when to quit and do something else.

A past issue of the *Journal of Medical Education* offers an excellent study of unsuccessful applicants to medical schools. Using questionnaires, the authors compiled data on a group of 98 rejected students. Information was solicited on the respondent's college major and accomplishments in the physical and biological sciences, MCAT scores, application patterns, the influence of various forces on the decision to enter medicine, the perceived reasons for rejection, and factors related to subsequent academic and career decisions. Of particular interest is the large percentage of rejected applicants who chose careers related to the health professions; i.e., dentist, podiatrist, optometrist, pharmacist, health educator, sanitary engineer, medical laboratory technician, medical and scientific writer, or pharmacologist.

In a similar study conducted at Johns Hopkins some interesting results were obtained. Almost 2,000 rejected applicants were questioned about their future plans. As explained in the "National Premedical Newsletter":

The majority of the 1,933 who responded to the questionnaire had reapplied to medical school. Of these, 27% had succeeded in entering either U.S. or foreign schools.

Since women comprised only 12.8% of the total applicant group, the entire available number of unaccepted female applicants was contacted. Of all who responded—men and women—most tended to have higher MCAT scores and were more likely to gain admission when they reapplied. Of the unaccepted applicants then engaged in study in foreign schools (96), 90% intended to practice in the U.S.

Among those who were rejected after a second try, many were still intending to reapply, a fact which would indicate that the original intention of becoming a doctor dies hard. It was found that the earlier in life the applicants had decided on a medical career, the less willing they were to give up, *especially if they had no "contingency plans."*

Most of those reapplying who sought counsel from unprofessional sources (family, friends) were urged to reapply and were more apt to do so. Such unprofessional advisers were not apt to suggest alternatives to a medical career.

What of those who did not reapply? The study found that 53% of the men and 42% of the women were still pursuing studies in graduate or professional schools, both in health-related and nonhealth-related fields. Of those pursuing studies other than medicine, but in health-related fields, 18% of the men were in dental school. The largest group of women were studying microbiology, bacteriology, or other medical sciences.

Most of the remaining group were employed, 55% of them in the health field—17% of the men and 31% of the women in clinical laboratory technology.

The doctors who conducted the survey were concerned that about half the unaccepted applicants are not being attracted to alternative health careers when there is such a vital need for additional health manpower in specific geographic areas and in particular aspects of health care. If this situation is to be turned around, the doctors felt that knowledgeable counselors should be available at the undergraduate and high school levels (rather than for the applicant to rely on family and friends *after* being turned down).

They also raised questions as to whether medical schools are selecting appropriate numbers and types of applicants in view of current and future health-care needs. Do the paramedical health careers need to be upgraded in terms of status and income to attract the appropriate personnel? They concluded that the answers to such questions will help determine the best use of this country's qualified health-oriented manpower.

Foreign study

For many rejected applicants, foreign medical schools offer an alternative to either giving up medicine or reapplying to U.S. medical schools. Currently, there are more than 10,000 U.S. medical students at school abroad. According to AAMC records, these students attend medical schools in some fifteen countries, chiefly Mexico, Italy, and the Dominican Republic. Small groups are located in Belgian, French, and Philippine medical schools. Medical schools in the United Kingdom and in Switzerland rarely accept U.S. students. In general, foreign schools using English as the language of instruction do not admit students from countries that have medical schools.

Some foreign medical schools have relatively "open" admission policies and request only transcripts, while others also require MCAT scores, a language examination, or competitive placement examination. Translations of transcripts are not always needed, and applicants should consult the Information Services or Consulate offices of the various foreign countries in the United States prior to preparing applications with supporting documents. Here is a list of several foreign government sources for medical school information:

Australia: Australian Consulate General
                     636 Fifth Avenue
                     New York, New York 10020

Austria: Austrian Information Service
                     31 East 69th Street
                     New York, New York 10021

Belgium: Executive Director
                     Commission for Education Exchange
                     Rue Marteau 21
                     1040 Brussels, Belgium

Great Britain: British Information Service
                     845 Third Avenue
                     New York, New York 10022

France: French Cultural Services
                     972 Fifth Avenue
                     New York, New York 10021

West Germany: German Academic Exchange Service
                     535 Fifth Avenue
                     New York, New York 10017

Italy: Italian Cultural Institute
                     686 Park Avenue
                     New York, New York 10021

Spain: Consulate General of Spain
                     150 East 58th Street
                     New York, New York 10155

New Zealand: New Zealand Consulate General
Suite 530
630 Fifth Avenue
New York, New York 10111

The trend in medical education in other countries, incidentally, predicts fewer rather than more places for U.S. citizens in the foreseeable future. Most foreign medical schools are state funded and must fulfill obligations to native citizens and applicants from underdeveloped nations without medical schools before a small percentage of places can be made available to U.S. citizens.

There are other reasons besides rejection from U.S. medical schools why Americans enroll abroad. Some have decided to begin medical school at an age when no U.S. medical school will accept them, notably in their early 40s. Others go for religious reasons, finding foreign schools more tolerant of certain beliefs and customs which would interfere with academic procedure in the U.S. Saturday classes, for example, impose a burden on Orthodox Jewish students in this country. Still others apply abroad feeling that their ethnic background discriminates against them here. The majority, however, may be said to have had low undergraduate grades, to have graduated without distinction, and to have been rejected by all the U.S. medical schools to which they applied.

The problems of studying medicine in a foreign country can be overwhelming. The language barrier is the main problem. Most foreign medical schools conduct their medical education programs in the language native to the country. In most places, the medical texts are also in that language. Any student considering studying abroad should find a country where the language is at least familiar, if not mastered already. Starting from scratch with a foreign language is hard enough without having to master medicine simultaneously.

Students studying abroad are on student visas and are rarely permitted to work to earn money. This means that if you go, you must be financed adequately before you embark. Although living costs are lower in some foreign countries, tuition can be comparable to that in the United States and travel expenses will be much higher. The cost of a foreign medical education can be in excess of $25,000 a year. Students from the United States may find themselves paying more than the natives for the same education. The assumption is that, because they are North American, they can afford it. In addition, many foreign medical schools do not meet the eligibility criteria for federally guaranteed student loans—another problem for financially pressed U.S. students.

Psychologically, the student from the U.S. is at a clear disadvantage in a foreign country. Having been rejected from U.S. schools and not having gone abroad as a first choice, the person in question is often embittered by what appears to be the AMA's stronghold over the medical profession in this country. Although culture shock may not be pronounced, being in a strange country is often an alienating experience. Unless there are other temporary expatriates to provide company, the American student abroad may initially experience overwhelming loneliness and frustration.

This attrition has been discussed with a number of American students and faculty in foreign schools and its causes have been generally determined. The largest number of Americans who opt out of foreign medical schools do so during their first year. The language handicap

Less than half the estimated number of U.S. citizens going to foreign medical schools return to this country as qualified physicians.

is undoubtedly the principal reason. At the European medical schools, where most examinations are oral, the foreign student's greatest weakness is the inability to express oneself. A student who survives the first year has an improved chance of lasting the entire medical course. After that first year, the dropout rate dips substantially. In the Swiss schools, students are permitted to repeat an examination in a given subject three times before they are finally dropped. In Italy, they have six chances; in Spain, five. Therefore some of the more tenacious students may take as many as eight years to complete a six-year course.

Many students who begin their medical studies abroad attempt to transfer to a U.S. medical school to complete their education. In 1980 approximately 11,000 students sought advanced placement in U.S. medical schools; about 370 were accepted. In 1988, only 133 gained acceptance. Most U.S. medical schools require students seeking advanced placement to take the Medical Science Knowledge Profile (MSKP), a test designed to provide the schools with a means of evaluating students' knowledge of medical sciences. The MSKP covers anatomy, behavioral sciences, biochemistry, introductory clinical diagnosis, microbiology, pathology, pharmacology, and physiology. The examination is given in June each year at selected test centers, and is administered over a two-day period. For further information on the MSKP write to: MSKP, Suite 301, 1776 Massachusetts Avenue, N.W., Washington, D.C. 20036.

"The language barrier is the main problem."

Perhaps the biggest problem in studying abroad is the uncertainty about what will happen afterwards. Most foreign schools are not approved by the AMA and graduates of these schools find it most difficult to get internships back home, even when there are shortages. The AMA is usually not in agreement with the teaching methods of foreign schools, or with the amount of clinical experience they offer their students. For this reason, students are often strongly urged to spend an extra year or two abroad interning before they return home to repeat their internship in U.S. hospitals. In addition, medical students educated abroad must pass a special examination developed by the Educational Commission for Foreign Medical Graduates. Good hospitals will not hire students who have not taken the test, for fear of incurring the wrath of the AMA, which supervises internships and residency programs in the United States.

I know of no evidence that it is any easier to get into an American medical school after a year abroad compared to taking an advanced degree or more course work, or simply reapplying. The choice of which path to follow is up to the individual. To recapitulate briefly, going to a foreign medical school is infinitely better than not going at all, especially if you are determined to become an MD. Graduate school should not be entered unless you sincerely want to earn a master's degree in one of the basic sciences. Extra course work should be followed to correct obvious weaknesses. Simply reapplying the next year is a prerogative reserved for the strongest applicants, who, I would suggest, should take the year off and enjoy themselves.

CHAPTER 7

Summer Programs for the Premed

Now that you've read the entire book and are a step ahead of the other students who haven't, there is one final important area to discuss. We have already stated that candidates who have worked in a medical environment are judged as being motivated and thought to make capable future physicians by admissions committee members. How then can you gain this valuable experience?

You have to go where the action is—to hospitals, laboratories, and research institutions. Summer employment at a medical center is fun, exciting, and educationally beneficial because it gives you a chance to see physicians and scientists at work. In addition, it may help to strengthen your career choices and to better define your own personal goals. This, in turn, will enable you to speak with some degree of authority about what medicine means to you and why you are contemplating such a career.

The following is a list of current summer programs that provide excellent opportunities to discover the world of medicine, learn laboratory procedures, and have a great summer too (some material is borrowed heavily from brochures describing individual programs):

1. Research Participation Program
   Roswell Park Memorial Institute
   666 Elm Street
   Buffalo, New York 14263

This is a program designed for students who have completed their junior year and who have research interests in science. The objectives of the program are "1) to expose the participant to an atmosphere of intensive research where he is in constant contact with scientists, and continually challenged by them, 2) to help develop his own scientific creativity, and 3) to aid in planning his career." Support for out-of-town students is currently a maximum of $60 a week; local students may receive a maximum of $40 a week. Inquiries should be directed to Dr. Edwin Mirand, Program Director, at the above address.

2. Summer Student Research Fellowship
   Department of Medical Education
   Hartford Hospital
   80 Seymour Street
   Hartford, Connecticut 06115

This is a ten-week program which commences on the first Monday in June and is under the chairmanship of Dr. Donald L. Brown. Up to fourteen first year summer fellowships are offered annually to qualified premedical students who will have completed at least three years of college. The program affords an opportunity to learn some of the methods of hospital research and patient treatment within the laboratory and clinical setting. Fellows will engage in an investigative program within a department division that is best suited to their medical and scientific interests. Research investigations are conducted under the guidance of full-time physicians in the Departments of Medicine (including the Divisions of Medical Research, Infectious Disease, Cardiology, Oncology, and Pulmonary), Obstetrics and Gynecology (Perinatology Division), Pathology (Hematology, Immunopathology and Microbiology Divisions), Pediatrics (Ambulatory, Cardiology, Infectious Disease, and Neonatology) and Surgery (ICU, Surgical Research, and Trauma). The fellowship stipend is $2000 for the first year and $2500 for the second year. Inquiries should be directed to Miss Marjorie Bingham, Director, Summer Student Fellowship Program.

3. Health Careers Opportunity Program
   New York University Medical Center
   Department of Rehabilitation Medicine
   400 East 34th Street
   New York, New York 10016

This program is conducted at the famous Rusk Institute in New York City. The fellowships are awarded in many basic research fields, social work, physical therapy, and clinical medicine. The program lasts for approximately one month and students receive a $300 stipend. In addition, students are entitled to use the library and other facilities of NYU and the Medical Center. Also, daily films and lectures are scheduled that deal with medically related topics and are uniformly interesting. Inquiries should be

directed to Mr. Glenn Goldfinger, Program Director, at
the address above. An asset of this program is the unique
opportunity to meet Dr. Howard Rusk and to learn about
a specific branch of medicine where compassion really
counts.

>4. Training and Education Office
> The Jackson Laboratory
> 600 Main Street
> Bar Harbor, Maine 04069

The core of the program is participation in biomedical
research under the guidance of a member of the laboratory's scientific staff. The greater part of each day is
devoted to the execution of a research project, with the
student working in the sponsor's laboratory or a nearby
laboratory. Students are exposed to all stages in the
development of a scientific experiment including its con-
ception and design, execution of the research plan, and
interpretation and communication of research results. The
balance between the amount of independent work and
supervised work by each student varies with the experience each participant brings to his or her project. The
research participation work is supplemented by lectures,
informal meetings with the staff, participation in discussion groups consisting of students and staff with mutual
research interests, and attendance at selected lectures in the
laboratory's annual short courses in genetics. A research
proposal is required of each participant at the end of the
first three weeks of the program. During the final days
of the program, the students present detailed oral and
written research papers. No examinations are given or
grades assigned during or at the conclusion of the program,
but certificates are presented to those who satisfactorily

meet the program requirements. In the past, several colleges have awarded credit toward a degree to their students who successfully participate in the program. A stipend, scholarship (to cover room and board and fees), and relocation allowance usually are provided. Inquiries should be directed to Training and Education Office at the above address.

> 5. Mellon Summer Research Program in
>   Psychiatry for Undergraduates
>   Western Psychiatric Institute and Clinic
>   3811 O'Hara Street
>   Pittsburgh, Pennsylvania 15213

The annual Mellon Summer Research Program in Psychiatry for undergraduates will provide six to eight fellowships to outstanding college juniors and seniors for an eight-week research experience in psychiatry that includes participation in clinical activities. This will involve close collaboration with faculty who are conducting investigations in clinical and basic psychiatric research. Fellowships are open to students with junior or senior standing by a specified date. Criteria for selection are the student's academic record, recommendations from two faculty members and a statement of objective describing the student's career goals and their relevance to this research program. Western Psychiatric Institute and Clinic, which houses the Department of Psychiatry of the University of Pittsburgh School of Medicine and is also the psychiatric specialty hospital of the University Health Center of Pittsburgh, provides a broad range of programs and activities dedicated to education, research, and patient care in western Pennsylvania. The institute offers

comprehensive continuity of care through inpatient-
outpatient services. Research at the institute focuses primarily upon developing methods and technology for the
diagnosis and treatment of severe mental disorders. The
stipend is $1200 plus travel expenses. Housing can be
arranged through the Western Psychiatric Institute and
Clinic. Inquiries should be directed to Dr. David Kupfer,
Director of Research, at the address indicated above.

6. The Hastings Center
   The Student Intern Program
   255 Elm Road
   Briarcliff Manor, NY 10510

The Hastings Center is an independent, nonprofit
research and educational organization that examines critical ethical issues in medicine, the life sciences, and the
professions. The student intern program is open to students actively pursuing a degree and interested in doing
serious and independent research. The interns are a mix
of students from professional schools, predominantly medicine and the law, and from the sciences and the humanities, including qualified undergraduates. However, the
research project must centrally focus on bioethical issues,
and the interns are expected to have adequate prior preparation in bioethics. Interns arrive throughout the year,
but most come in the summer or during the January
break. The students are assigned to specific staff associates
who oversee the progress of their work, which generally
involves a final paper. Interns are invited to participate
in the center's daily life, including project meetings and
luncheon discussions. The length of an internship, except
for advanced graduate or professional students, is from

two weeks to one month. There are no stipends or fellow-ships. Applications for the summer are due by April 15 and for January, by November 15. Direct inquiries to the Director of Education at the address above.

7. **Surgery Laboratory Program**
   Baylor College of Medicine
   Texas Medical Center
   Houston, Texas 77030

This is a fascinating program which offers undergrad-uates an opportunity to view surgical procedures, study pathological specimens, and assist in animal operations. The program is under the titular direction of Dr. M. DeBakey in the Cora and Webb Mading Department of Surgery at Baylor College of Medicine in Houston, Texas. Financial remuneration is limited as are the number of student places available. However, interested students should contact Mr. Craig Fredrickson, Administrative Assistant, Department of Surgery at the address above.

8. Summer Student Research Fellowship
   Program
   Dr. James Magner
   Division of Endocrinology
   Michael Reese Medical Center
   29th Street and Ellis Avenue
   Chicago, Illinois 60616

The world-famous Michael Reese Medical Center spon-sors a ten-week summer research program for qualified undergraduate students interested in the possibility of a medical career. A specific research project is proposed by the sponsor and a single student is assigned to that project. The stipend for the summer is approximately $1500. Interested students should write to the Program Director at the above address. Deadline for applications is December 15.

9. Summer Scientific Work Program
   Franklin General Hospital
   900 Franklin Avenue
   Valley Stream, New York 11580

This program is conducted at a 425-bed, acute care and chronic community hospital. It gained acclaim when it was reviewed in the prestigious *Journal of Medical Education*. Students "shadow" physicians on rounds in the hospital and perform various laboratory procedures. Lectures and demonstrations are an integral part of the program and a small stipend is available. The program is open to sophomores and juniors who reside in the hospital's service community; they should contact Mr. Albert Dicker, Executive Director, for further information.

10. Health Policy Advisory Center
    Health/PAC
    17 Murray Street
    New York, New York 10007

The Health Policy Advisory Center is an organization that conducts independent health-related research on the social issues of medicine. The "Health/PAC" bulletin is a widely read journal that covers such topics as insurance, malpractice, and hospital financing. Both offices of the organization will sponsor interested students who wish to conduct original research and to help write articles for the bulletin. Although no stipend is available, this could be a very worthwhile experience especially for students interested in community-related health problems. Inquiries should be directed to the office listed and should include a resume and a one-page description of proposed research project.

>   11. Mental Health Internship
>   Psychiatric Institute
>   4460 MacArthur Boulevard, N.W.
>   Washington, D.C. 20007

This is a summer internship geared toward undergraduates interested in the field of mental health. It is a ten-week program conducted at the Psychiatric Institute in Washington, D.C. Application dates are January through March 15 of each year. Approximately 125 candidates apply each year. Initial screening and final selection rests with the Department of Education at the Psychiatric Institute. Interested students should contact the Director at the above address.

>   12. Personnel Department
>   University of California
>   Lawrence Livermore Laboratory
>   Post Office Box 808-N
>   Livermore, California 94550

Each year the Lawrence Livermore Laboratory in Livermore, California, offers summer appointments to students from colleges and universities across the country.

These appointments are normally for the period of regular school vacation. The program has a two-fold objective. First, it permits such summer employees to apply their academic backgrounds to practical research problems resulting in worthwhile work experience. Second, it benefits the laboratory by bringing new ideas and fresh approaches to current scientific research problems. Assignments for summer appointees are distributed among all of the major departments and research programs. It is expected that there will be openings in experimental physics, theoretical physics, computer programming, chemistry, biology and medicine, and hazards control. Supplementary brochures describing the work of these groups in more detail may be obtained through the placement office. Undergraduate and graduate students should submit an application and a complete college transcript or an unofficial list of courses and credits, including current courses. In addition, students should ask two faculty members familiar with their records to submit confidential statements (references) to the laboratory. We suggest that students also provide brief statements of their technical interests and assignment preferences. Application forms may be obtained from the placement office or by writing directly to the laboratory.

13. Office of Educational Programs
Brookhaven National Laboratory
Upton, New York 11973

The Brookhaven National Laboratory sponsors a summer student program supported by the U.S. Department of Energy. Applicants must be 18 years of age or older and have completed their junior year of college. Students work with members of the scientific staff and gain research experience in biology, physics, chemistry, medicine, engineering, and mathematics. The laboratory provides a stipend of $200 per week plus round-trip travel and on-site housing expenses. Brookhaven has an international reputation for excellence and any position at the laboratory would be highly regarded in medical spheres. Inquiries should be sent to Dr. Donald J. Metz at the above address.

These thirteen internships and research positions should interest many premedical students from numerous colleges and universities. If you are unsuccessful in obtaining entrance to these programs, as they are becoming more competitive, here are some other words of advice from the Career Planning Offices of Bryn Mawr and Haverford colleges:

Look in the phone book for a list of hospitals and then send away for information from those hospitals which interest you. Ask them if they sponsor internships, research-oriented or otherwise, for undergraduates, or if they are willing to hire you, or accept you as a volunteer, for some position in their hospital. It may not be an internship, but it is an excellent way to become familiar with hospitals, medicine, and what the discipline of medicine requires from those who practice it.

Another worthwhile reference source is the journals of the various health professions. Thumb through these journals, looking specifically for articles describing an ongoing research program which might be of interest to you. Write down the name of the people conducting the research and the address of the institution sponsoring the research project and mail them a letter stating your interest in their program, telling how you heard about it, and asking whether they sponsor internships or would like to hire someone with your qualifications.

Remember to point out that you are interested in a medical career and hope to gain something out of the classroom or "real world" experiences. Be honest and you'll be surprised at the warmth of the reactions you'll receive.

CHAPTER **8**

Directory of American Medical Schools

The following directory of American medical schools provides a beginning for your search for a medical school. These schools are all accredited by the Liaison Committee on Medical Education (LCME), an accrediting agency which is sponsored by the Association of American Medical Colleges and the American Medical Association.

I extend my gratitude to the admission committee members who took the time to complete the questionnaire I sent them. For additional information on admissions policies and programs of study at these schools, you should check *Medical School Admission Requirements: United States and Canada,* 1989–90 edition, published by the Association of American Medical Colleges, Washington, D.C., and the *AAMC Curriculum Directory* and the *AAMC Directory of Medical Education,* also published annually by the AAMC.

Schools have been designated by their membership in AMCAS (see p. 66 for complete explanation) and/or in WICHE, the Western Interstate Commission for Higher

Education, a 13-state student exchange program under which students from Alaska, Idaho, Montana, and Wyoming can attend the participating schools and pay only the in-state tuition at a public school or a reduced fee at a private school.

Each profile in the directory includes the following data:

- The correct name and address of the medical school; whether the New MCAT is required for admission.
- Both the overall GPA and the science GPA, if available.
- Information about the medical school: the founding date; under public or private control; any special programs.
- Enrollment data and costs, in approximate figures.
- Information about the application, notification, and response dates; amount of deposit; early decision plan; state residency preference; admissions criteria; and the person or office to whom admissions correspondence should be sent.
- Information about minority students, including percentage of the total and first-year student classes, percentage receiving aid, special programs, aid application deadlines, and the person or office to whom aid inquiries may be addressed; the application fee.

Accredited Schools

Albany Medical College*
47 New Scotland Avenue
Albany, NY 12208

NEW MCAT: required

GPA: overall 3.2

FOUNDED 1839; *private.* The Medical College, in conjunction with Rensselaer Polytechnic Institute, sponsors the Accelerated Biomedical Program, a six-year program leading to the B.S. and M.D. degrees.

ENROLLMENT: 340 men, 175 woman (total); 75 men, 55 women (first-year).

COSTS: tuition $17,000, other expenses $6800.

APPLICATIONS should be submitted between June 15 and December 1; the application fee is $50. Notification begins October 1; response must be received within 2 weeks; $100 deposit required to reserve place in class. In recent years, approximately 70% of entering students have been state residents. Admission factors include academic record, New MCAT scores, and personal qualifications as evaluated from letters of recommendation and a personal interview. *Correspondence to:* Director of Admissions.

MINORITY STUDENTS comprise 3% of the total student enrollment, 7% of the first-year class; most of these students receive aid. The $50 application fee may be waived. The Medical College offers a special orientation program and introduction to the basic Medical Sciences for entering students who exhibit special academic needs. Tutorial assistance is available during the academic year. *For additional information:* Office of Minority Affairs. Information regarding application for financial assistance is made available March 1.

* member AMCAS

121

Albert Einstein College of Medicine
of Yeshiva University*
1300 Morris Park Avenue
Bronx, NY 10461

NEW MCAT: required

GPA: 3.4 overall

FOUNDED 1955; *private.*

ENROLLMENT: 400 men, 310 women (total); 100 men, 85 women (first-year).

COSTS: tuition $17,000, student fees $600, other expenses $6600.

APPLICATIONS should be submitted between June 15 and November 15; the application fee is $60. Notification begins January 15; response must be received within two weeks until May 1, within one week thereafter; $100 deposit needed to hold place in class. Early Decision plan is available. While no strict preference is given to state residents, about 70% of the entering class have been New York residents in recent years. Admission criteria include academic performance, MCAT results, letters of recommendation, and personal qualifications as judged by the Committee on Admissions. *Correspondence to:* Admissions Officer.

MINORITY STUDENTS comprise 10% of the total student body, 13% of the first-year class; most of these students receive aid. Applications received from minority students are considered by a subcommittee of the Committee on Admissions. *For additional information:* Director, Special Education Programs. Applications for aid are available upon acceptance.

* member AMCAS

Baylor College of Medicine
One Baylor Plaza
Houston, TX 77030

NEW MCAT: required

GPA: 3.6 overall

FOUNDED 1900, moved to Houston in 1947; *private.* Optional three-year program, requiring special approval, is available.

ENROLLMENT: 450 men, 200 women (total); 115 men, 55 women (first-year).

COSTS: tuition $4500 ($16,500 out-of-state), student fees $1250; other expenses $12,100.

APPLICATIONS should be submitted between June 15 and November 1; the application fee is $35. Notification begins October 15; response must be received within two weeks; $300 deposit needed to secure a position in the class. Early Decision plan is available. Some preference is given to state residents; 70% of a recent freshman class were residents of Texas. Admission factors include collegiate curriculum and performance, New MCAT scores, and personal qualifications as evaluated in letters of recommendation and the personal interview. *Correspondence to:* Office of Admissions.

MINORITY STUDENTS comprise 6% of the total student enrollment, 4% of the first-year class; most of these students receive aid. The $35 application fee may be waived. A special minority subcommittee of the Admissions Committee reviews all applications from minority students. The College of Medicine also sponsors a summer work-study program for minority premedical students. *For additional information:* Associate Dean. Applications for aid should be requested within two weeks of submission of application.

Boston University*
School of Medicine
80 East Concord Street
Boston, MA 02118

NEW MCAT: required

GPA: 3.5 overall

FOUNDED 1848 as the New England Female Medical College; *private*. Special programs include a six-year Liberal Arts–Medical Education Program which admits students after the senior year of high school.

ENROLLMENT: 365 men, 240 women (total); 85 men, 60 women (first-year).

COSTS: tuition $21,500, student fees $50, other expenses $12,100.

APPLICATIONS should be submitted between June 15 and November 15; the application fee is $50. Notification begins November 1; response must be received within 2 weeks; no deposit needed to hold place in class. Early Decision plan is available. Selection factors include scholastic record, college recommendations, involvement in college and community activities, as well as personal qualifications. *Correspondence to:* Admissions Office.

MINORITY STUDENTS comprise 10% of the total student body, 10% of the first-year class; most of these students are receiving aid. The $50 application fee may be waived. The Office of Minority Affairs organizes programs for the recruitment and support of minority students. These include a special prematriculation summer program in the medical sciences. *For additional information:* Assistant Dean for Minority Affairs.

* member AMCAS

**Bowman Gray School of Medicine
of Wake Forest University***
300 South Hawthorne Road
Winston-Salem, NC 27103

NEW MCAT: required

GPA: 3.4 overall

FOUNDED 1902 as two-year school, became four-year
school in 1941; *private.* A new Parallel Curriculum is
problem, rather than discipline, based and emphasizes
critical thinking and clinical reasoning.

ENROLLMENT: 285 men, 140 women (total); 75 men, 40
women (first-year).

COSTS: tuition and fees, $10,850, other expenses $8600.

APPLICATIONS should be submitted between June 15 and
November 1; the application fee is $40. Notification be-
gins November 1; response must be received by school
within two weeks; $100 deposit needed to hold place in
class. Admissions decisions are based on the New
MCAT, GPA, letters of recommendation, interview, and
personal characteristics. *Correspondence to:* Office of
Medical School Admissions.

MINORITY STUDENTS comprise 4% of the total student body;
4% of first-year students. A summer program is available
to entering minority students. *For additional information:* Director of Minority Affairs.

* member AMCAS

Brown University
Program in Medicine
97 Waterman Street
Providence, RI 02912

NEW MCAT: required only for the MD-PhD program

GPA: not available

FOUNDED 1973; *private.* Eight-year combined B.A.-M.D.
program; certain students also accepted to 4-year de-
gree-granting program, entering in the fourth year of the
8-year program. Students in the Brown-Dartmouth Medical Program spend the first 2 years at Dartmouth and
the last 2 years at Brown.

ENROLLMENT: 160 men, 130 women (total); 35 men, 25
women (first-year).

COSTS: tuition $16,300, student fees $550, other expenses
$7100.

APPLICATIONS should be submitted between August 15 and
November 1; the application fee is $60. Notification be-
gins November 1; response must be received within
three weeks; a deposit of $100 is required to hold place
in class. Admission factors weighted most heavily include GPA, background in the humanities or social sciences, letters of recommendation and the interview.
Correspondence to: Office of Admissions, Box G.

MINORITY STUDENTS comprise 9% of the total student body,
approximately 10% of the first-year class. *For additional
information:* Assistant Dean of Medicine for Minority
Affairs. Application for aid should be made upon acceptance.

Case Western Reserve University*
School of Medicine
2119 Abington Road
Cleveland, OH 44106

NEW MCAT: required

GPA: 3.4

FOUNDED 1843; *private.*

ENROLLMENT: 310 men, 250 women (total); 80 men, 60 women (first-year).

COSTS: tuition $14,800, student fees $350, other expenses $9,200.

APPLICATIONS should be submitted between June 15 and November 15; the application fee is $30. Notification begins October 15; response must be received within 1 month; no deposit needed to hold place in class. Early Decision plan is available. Preference is given to state residents. Admission factors include academic performance, MCAT results, verbal skills, letters of recommendation, and the personal interview. *Correspondence to:* Associate Dean for Admissions.

MINORITY STUDENTS comprise 8% of the total student body, 13% of the first-year class; 90% of these students receive aid. *For additional information:* Office of Minority Programs.

* member AMCAS

Columbia University
College of Physicians and Surgeons
630 West 168th Street
New York City, NY 10032

NEW MCAT: required

GPA: not available

FOUNDED 1767; *private.*

ENROLLMENT: 395 men, 215 women (total); 80 men, 65 women (first-year).

COSTS: tuition $15,800, student fees $650, other expenses $9300.

APPLICATIONS should be submitted between June 15 and October 15; application fee is $50. Notification begins February 1; response must be received within three weeks; no deposit required to hold place in class. Twice as many residents as nonresidents are accepted. Admission factors include academic record, letters of recommendation, the personal interview, nonacademic achievements and activities, and personal qualifications. *Correspondence to:* Admissions Office.

MINORITY STUDENTS comprise 9% of the total student enrollment, 8% of the first-year class. Tutorial assistance is available to all students who require such help. *For additional information:* Director, Office of Minority Affairs.

Cornell University Medical College*
1300 York Avenue
New York City, NY 10021

NEW MCAT: required

GPA: 3.6 science, 3.7 overall

FOUNDED 1898; *private.*

ENROLLMENT: 240 men, 155 women (total); 65 men, 35 women (first-year).

COSTS: tuition and fees $17,200, other expenses $7900.

APPLICATIONS should be submitted between June 15 and November 1; the application fee is $50. Notification begins October 15; response must be received within 2 weeks; $100 deposit needed to reserve place in class. Early Decision plan is available. In recent years, about one-half of the entering class have been New York state residents. Admission factors include academic records, letters of evaluation, personal qualifications, extracurricular activities, and the personal interview. *Correspondence to:* Office of Admissions.

MINORITY STUDENTS comprise 17% of the total enrollment, 13% of the first-year class. The $50 application fee may be waived. The Medical College sponsors a summer fellowship program for about 20 minority group premedical students who have completed their junior year. *For additional information:* Associate Dean, Equal Opportunity Programs. Application for aid should be made upon acceptance.

* member AMCAS

Creighton University*
School of Medicine
California at 24th Street
Omaha, NE 68178

NEW MCAT: required

GPA: 3.3 overall, 3.2 science

FOUNDED 1892; *private.*

ENROLLMENT: 340 men, 115 women (total); 85 men, 40 women (first-year).

COSTS: tuition $13,500, student fees $400, other expenses $7300.

APPLICATIONS should be submitted between June 15 and December 15; application fee is $40. Notification begins October 15; response must be received within 2 weeks; $100 deposit needed to hold place in class. Early Decision plan is available. Some preference is given to residents of midwestern states and residents of those states without medical schools. Admission factors counted heavily include GPA, New MCAT, and recommendations from academic professors or premedical committee. *Correspondence to:* Health Sciences Admissions Office.

MINORITY STUDENTS comprise 7% of the total enrollment, 10% of the first-year class; most of these students are receiving aid; most of those who enter remain to graduate. The $50 application fee may be waived. *For additional information:* Arlene Rhodes, Director of Minority Affairs. Submit application for financial aid after acceptance.

* member AMCAS

Dartmouth Medical School*
Hanover, NH 03756

NEW MCAT: required

GPA: not available

FOUNDED 1797; *private.* Students in a special program spend the first 2 years at Dartmouth and then transfer to Brown University for the last 2 years.

ENROLLMENT: 145 men, 165 women (total); 35 men, 50 women (first-year)

COSTS: tuition $17,500, student fees $500, other expenses $7200.

APPLICATIONS should be submitted between June 15 and November 1; the application fee is $65. Notification begins December 15. Response must be received within 2 weeks of notification; no deposit needed to hold place in class. Early Decision plan is available. Some preference is given to applicants from northern New England. Admission factors include consideration of both academic and personal qualifications. *Correspondence to:* Office of Admissions.

MINORITY STUDENTS comprise 8% of the total enrollment, 7% of the first-year class. The $65 application fee may be waived. The Committee on Equal Opportunity, which includes minority students and faculty members, is involved in the evaluation and selection of minority applicants. *For additional information:* Assistant Dean, Admissions and Financial Aid. Application for aid should be made upon acceptance.

* member AMCAS

Duke University*
School of Medicine
P.O. Box 3710
Durham, NC 27710

NEW MCAT: required

GPA: not available

FOUNDED 1930; *private.*

ENROLLMENT: 320 men, 145 women (total); 70 men, 35 women (first-year).

COSTS: tuition $12,300, student fees $750, other expenses $7700.

APPLICATIONS should be submitted between June 15 and November 1; the application fee is $50 for nonresidents. Notification begins October 1; response must be received by school within three weeks; $50 deposit needed to hold place in class. The School of Medicine reserves 30 places for in-state students. Admission factors include academic record, New MCAT results, extracurricular activities, faculty evaluations, and the personal interview. *Correspondence to:* Committee on Admissions.

MINORITY STUDENTS comprise 6% of the total enrollment, 10% of the first-year class; almost all of these students receive aid. The $50 nonresident application fee may be waived. Minority group faculty and students are included in the membership of the Committee on Admissions. *For additional information:* Associate Dean, Medical Education. Application materials for financial aid are available upon acceptance.

* member AMCAS

East Carolina University*
School of Medicine
Greenville, NC 27858

NEW MCAT: required

GPA: 3.3 overall

FOUNDED 1977; *publicly controlled.*

ENROLLMENT: 190 men, 85 women (total); 50 men, 35 women (first-year).

COSTS: tuition $1150 ($8200 out-of-state), student fees $500, other expenses $5700.

APPLICATIONS should be submitted between June 15 and December 1; the application fee is $15. Notification begins October 15; response must be received within 3 weeks; $100 deposit needed to hold place in class. Early Decision plan is available. Preference is given to state residents. Admission factors include academic record, New MCAT scores, and personal qualifications as evaluated in letters of recommendation and two personal interviews. *Correspondence to:* Associate Dean, Office of Admissions and Student Affairs.

MINORITY STUDENTS comprise 12% of the total student enrollment, 15% of the first-year class. *For additional information:* Director, Center for Student Opportunities.

* member AMCAS

Eastern Virginia Medical School*
700 Olney Road
P.O. Box 1980
Norfolk, VA 23501

NEW MCAT: required

GPA: 3.2 overall, 3.2 science

FOUNDED 1973; *private.*

ENROLLMENT: 220 men, 150 women (total); 50 men, 45 women (first-year).

COSTS: tuition $10,500 ($16,000 out-of-state), student fees $600, other expenses $8800.

APPLICATIONS should be submitted between June 15 and January 15; the application fee is $50. Notification begins October 15; response must be received within 10 days; $200 deposit needed to hold place in class. Early Decision plan is available. Preference given to state residents, particularly applicants from the Hampton Roads area of Virginia. Admission criteria include academic achievement, New MCAT results, written evaluation, personal interview, and evidence of sustained motivation. *Correspondence to:* Office of Admissions.

MINORITY STUDENTS comprise 5% of the total student enrollment, 5% of the first-year class; almost all of these students receive aid. The $50 application fee may be waived. The Medical School sponsors a remedial assistance program for students requiring such help during the academic year. *For additional information:* Assistant Dean, Minority and Women's Affairs. Applications for aid should be submitted by April 1.

* member AMCAS

East Tennessee State University*
Quillen-Dishner College of Medicine
P.O. Box 19900A
Johnson City, TN 37614

NEW MCAT: required

GPA: 3.3 overall

FOUNDED 1974; *publicly controlled.*

ENROLLMENT: 155 men, 65 women (total); 40 men, 20 women (first-year).

COSTS: tuition $5900 ($9400 out-of-state), student fees $350, other expenses $7500.

APPLICATIONS should be submitted between June 15 and December 1; the application fee is $15. Notification begins October 15; response must be received within 2 weeks; $100 deposit needed to hold place in class. Early Decision plan is available. Preference is given to state residents. Selection factors include both academic and personal qualifications. *Correspondence to:* Admissions Officer/Registrar.

MINORITY STUDENTS comprise 10% of the total student body, 15% of the first-year class. *For additional information:* Assistant Dean, Student Affairs.

* member AMCAS

Emory University*
School of Medicine
Woodruff Health Sciences Center Administration
    Building
Atlanta, GA 30322

NEW MCAT: required

GPA: 3.6 overall

FOUNDED 1915; *private.*

ENROLLMENT: 295 men, 150 women (total); 75 men, 40
women (first-year).

COSTS: tuition $12,800, student fees $300, other expenses
$7600.

APPLICATIONS should be submitted between June 15 and
October 15; the application fee is $40. Notification be-
gins October 15; response must be received within 3
weeks; $50 deposit needed to hold place in class. Pref-
erence given to state residents; approximately one-half
of the entering students are Georgia residents. The remaining positions are filled by out-of-state applicants,
with some preference for residents of the southeastern
states. Selection factors include academic performance,
fitness and aptitude for the study of medicine, and personal qualifications. *Correspondence to:* Medical
School Admissions, Room 303, Woodruff Health Sciences Center Administration Building.

MINORITY STUDENTS comprise 6% of total student enrollment, 9% of the first-year class; most of these students
receive aid. The $40 application fee may be waived. *For
additional information:* Director, Office of Minority Affairs. Applications for aid should be submitted upon acceptance.

* member AMCAS

Georgetown University*
School of Medicine
3900 Reservoir Road, N.W.
Washington, DC 20007

NEW MCAT: required

GPA: 3.4 overall

FOUNDED 1851; *private.*

ENROLLMENT: 580 men, 245 women (total); 135 men, 70 women (first-year).

COSTS: tuition $22,500, other expenses $9900.

APPLICATIONS should be submitted between June 15 and November 15; the application fee is $50. Notification begins November 1; response must be received within 2 weeks; $100 deposit required to hold place in class. Early Decision plan is available. Admission factors include scholastic record, New MCAT scores, personal qualifications, letters of recommendation, and the personal interview. *Correspondence to:* Office of Admissions.

MINORITY STUDENTS comprise 7% of the total student enrollment, 11% of the first-year class; most of these students receive aid. The $50 application fee may be waived. A summer enrichment program is offered to strengthen the backgrounds of students entering in the fall. *For additional information:* Dr. Arthur H. Hoyte, Director, Office of Programs for Student Development and Community Affairs. Application for aid should be made upon acceptance.

* member AMCAS

The George Washington University*
School of Medicine and Health Sciences
2300 Eye Street, N.W.
Washington, DC 20037

NEW MCAT: required

GPA: 3.3 overall

FOUNDED 1825; *private*.

ENROLLMENT: 385 men, 230 women (total); 90 men, 55 women (first-year).

COSTS: tuition $22,000, student fees $200, other expenses $9800.

APPLICATIONS should be submitted between June 15 and December 1; the application fee is $40. Notification begins October 15; response must be received within 3 weeks; no deposit is needed to hold place in class. Early Decision plan is available. Some preference is given to residents of the District of Columbia and the surrounding metropolitan area. Admission factors include academic record, trends in performance, New MCAT scores, extracurricular activities and work experiences, letter of recommendation, the personal interview, and the essay portion of the application. *Correspondence to:* Office of Admissions.

MINORITY STUDENTS comprise 3% of the total student body, 4% of the first-year class; more than half of these students are receiving aid. The $40 application fee may be waived. Tutorial assistance is available to all students who require help. Minority students and faculty members serve on the Committee on Admissions. *For additional information:* Associate Dean for Student Affairs and Admissions. Financial aid information and applications are available upon acceptance.

* member AMCAS

Hahnemann University*
School of Medicine
Broad and Vine Streets
Philadelphia, PA 19102-1192

NEW MCAT: required

GPA: 3.3 overall, 3.4 science

FOUNDED 1848; *private.*

ENROLLMENT: 460 men, 210 women (total); 125 men, 65 women (first-year).

COSTS: tuition $16,650, student fees $700, other expenses $8600.

APPLICATIONS should be submitted between June 15 and November 15; the application fee is $50. Notification begins October 15; response must be received by school within 15 days; $100 deposit needed to hold place in class. Early Decision plan is available. Preference is given to state residents. Selection factors include academic achievement, New MCAT scores, and personal qualifications as attested by recommendations and the personal interview. *Correspondence to:* Medical School Admissions.

MINORITY STUDENTS comprise 11% of the total student body, 17% of the first-year class; most of these students receive aid. The $50 application fee may be waived. The flexible curriculum permits students of educationally disadvantaged backgrounds to divide the first-year curriculum into two years to aid in their academic adjustment. The Medical College also sponsors a pre-enrollment Summer Academic Enrichment Program, and a tutorial assistance program. *For additional information:* Director, The Resource System.

* member AMCAS

Harvard Medical School
25 Shattuck Street
Boston, MA 02115

NEW MCAT: required

GPA: not available

FOUNDED 1782; *private.*

ENROLLMENT: 425 men, 240 women (total); 105 men, 55 women (first-year).

COSTS: tuition $15,500, student fees $1200, other expenses $9100.

APPLICATION request must be received prior to October 1; applications should be submitted between May 1 and October 15; the application fee, due with request for application, is $55. Response after notification must be received within 3 weeks; no deposit needed to hold place in class. Admission criteria include the New MCAT, extracurricular activities, summer occupations, and letters of recommendation. Also considered are personal integrity, judgment, maturity and aptitude. *Correspondence to:* Director of Admissions.

MINORITY STUDENTS comprise 14% of the total student body, 13% of the first-year class. Some tutorial assistance is available to those in need of such help. *For additional information:* Dr. Alvin F. Poussaint, Associate Dean for Student Affairs. Application for aid should be made upon acceptance.

Howard University*
College of Medicine
520 W Street, N.W.
Washington, DC 20059

NEW MCAT: required

GPA: 3.1 overall, 3.0 science

FOUNDED 1868; *private (federal government supported).*
Special programs include the Shortened Medical Curriculum Program, a three-year program leading to the
M.D. degree; the Early Entry Medical Education Program, which admits students after two or three years of
college work; and a six-year combined B.S.-M.D. program.

ENROLLMENT: 225 men, 190 women (total); 55 men, 50
women (first-year).

COSTS: tuition $7100, student fees $750, other expenses
$10,400.

APPLICATIONS should be submitted between June 15 and
December 15; the application fee is $25. Notification
begins October 15; response must be received within
one month; $100 deposit needed to reserve place in
class. Admission factors include academic record, New
MCAT scores, motivation and personal qualifications,
letters of recommendation, and an interview. *Correspondence to:* Admissions Office.

MINORITY STUDENTS comprise 68% of the total study body,
60% of the first-year class; women comprise 46% of the
total enrollment, 45% of the first-year class. Most receive
aid. *For additional information:* Sterling M. Lloyd, Jr.,
Assistant Dean, Student Affairs.

* member AMCAS

Indiana University*
School of Medicine
1120 South Drive
Indianapolis, IN 46223

NEW MCAT: required

GPA: 3.7 overall

FOUNDED 1903; *publicly controlled.* The University
School of Medicine has first- and second-year medical
programs on seven college campuses in the state.

ENROLLMENT: 725 men, 340 women (total); 190 men, 85
women (first-year).

COSTS: tuition $4700 ($10,800 out-of-state).

APPLICATIONS should be submitted between June 15 and
December 15; the application fee is $20. Notification
begins November 15; response must be received within
3 weeks; no deposit needed to hold place in class. Early
Decision plan is available. Strong preference is given to
state residents; recently, less than 5% of the entering
class are nonresidents. Admission criteria include the
New MCAT, scholarship, character, and residence. *Correspondence to:* Medical School Admissions Office, Fes-
ler Hall 213.

MINORITY STUDENTS comprise 2% of the total student body,
2% of the first-year class; tutorial and financial assistance
are available. *For additional information:* Associate
Dean for Student and Curricular Affairs.

* member AMCAS

**Jefferson Medical College
of Thomas Jefferson University***
1025 Walnut Street
Philadelphia, PA 19107

NEW MCAT: required

GPA: 3.6 overall, 3.5 science

FOUNDED 1824; *private, with state support.* The Cooperative Five-Year Program in Medicine with the Pennsylvania State University leads to a combined B.S.-M.D. degree in 6 calendar years; the Physician Shortage Area Program is designed to recruit and educate medical students to enter family medicine and practice in rural communities and inner cities of Pennsylvania (physician-shortage areas).

ENROLLMENT: 590 men, 300 women (total); 140 men, 90 women (first-year). Up to 40 places in each class may be filled from the Cooperative Five-Year Program; 20 more places are usually set aside for Delaware residents through a special program with the state.

COSTS: tuition $15,600, student fees $50, other expenses $9600.

APPLICATIONS should be submitted between June 15 and November 15; the application fee is $60. Notification begins November 15; response must be received within 2 weeks; $100 deposit needed to hold place in class. Early Decision plan is available. Preference is given to state residents. Admission factors include consideration of undergraduate college attended, academic performance, New MCAT scores, letters of recommendation, and a personal interview. *Correspondence to:* Associate Dean for Admissions.

MINORITY STUDENTS comprise 5% of the total student body, 10% of the first-year class; most of these students receive aid. Application for aid should be made by April 1. *For additional information:* Associate Dean for Student and Minority Affairs.

* member AMCAS

144

The Johns Hopkins University
School of Medicine
720 Rutland Avenue
Baltimore, MD 21205

NEW MCAT: not required

GPA: not available

FOUNDED 1893; *private*. In addition to the four-year program, an optional three-year program is offered. There is also a five-year B.A.-M.D. Human Biology Program designed for students who have completed two years of college work.

ENROLLMENT: 305 men, 160 women (total); 75 men, 40 women (first-year).

COSTS: tuition $14,000, student fees $850, other expenses $10,700.

APPLICATIONS should be submitted between July 1 and November 15; the application fee is $50. Notification begins November 15; response must be received within 2 weeks; no deposit needed to hold place in class. Early Decision plan is available. Admission factors include academic record, MCAT scores, extracurricular activities, and personal qualifications. *Correspondence to:* Committee on Admission.

MINORITY STUDENTS comprise 10% of the total study body, 7% of the first-year class. An advising system is available to students which permits the selection of both preclinical and clinical faculty advisors. A faculty member is also designated as minority student advisor. *For additional information:* Dr. Roland T. Smoot, Assistant Dean for Student Affairs.

Loma Linda University*†
School of Medicine
Loma Linda, CA 92354

NEW MCAT: required

GPA: 3.6 overall

FOUNDED 1909; *privately controlled.* Seventh-Day Adventist Church.

ENROLLMENT: 405 men, 165 women (total); 95 men, 50 women (first-year).

COSTS: tuition $14,250, other expenses $8700.

APPLICATIONS should be submitted between June 15 and November 15; the application fee is $35. Notification begins December 15; response must be received within 1 month; $100 deposit needed to hold place in class. Preference is given to Seventh-Day Adventists. Admission factors include GPA, New MCAT scores, letters of recommendation, and the personal interview. *Correspondence to:* Associate Dean for Admissions.

MINORITY STUDENTS comprise 6% of total enrollment, 6% of first-year class. The $35 application fee may be waived. *For additional information:* Associate Dean, Student Affairs.

* member AMCAS
† member WICHE

Louisiana State University*
School of Medicine in New Orleans
1542 Tulane Avenue
New Orleans, LA 70112

NEW MCAT: required

GPA: 3.3 overall, 3.4 science

FOUNDED 1931; *publicly controlled.*

ENROLLMENT: 485 men, 210 women (total); 130 men, 55 women (first-year).

COSTS: tuition $4750, other expenses $9100.

APPLICATIONS should be submitted between June 15 and November 15; the application fee is $30. Notification begins November 15; response must be received within 2 weeks; no deposit needed to hold place in class. Strong preference is given to state residents; recently 100% of the entering class were Louisiana residents. Admission factors include the New MCAT, scholastic performance, extracurricular activities, character, attitude, and interest. *Correspondence to:* Admissions Office.

MINORITY STUDENTS comprise 7% of the total student body, 8% of the first-year class. A broad program of student aid is administered by the Student Financial Aid Office to help students financially through awards, scholarships, and loans. *For additional information:* Coordinator, Minority Affairs.

* member AMCAS

Louisiana State University*
School of Medicine in Shreveport
P.O. Box 33932
Shreveport, LA 71130

NEW MCAT: required

GPA: 3.4 overall, 3.4 science

FOUNDED 1965, admitted first class in 1969; *publicly controlled.* The School of Medicine, in conjunction with LSU in Shreveport, also sponsors a six-year combined program leading to the baccalaureate and M.D. degrees, in addition to its four-year program.

ENROLLMENT: 290 men, 90 women (total); 80 men, 30 women (first-year).

COSTS: tuition $4550, student fees $100, other expenses $12,400.

APPLICATIONS should be submitted between June 15 and November 15; the application fee is $30. Notification begins November 15; response must be received within 2 weeks; $100 deposit needed to hold place in class. Strong preference given to state residents. In recent years, admission has been limited to Louisiana residents. Selection factors include academic record, New MCAT scores, recommendations, and personal interviews. *Correspondence to:* Office of Student Admissions, LSU Medical Center.

MINORITY STUDENTS comprise 7% of the total student body, 10% of the first-year class; most of these students receive aid. The $30 application fee may be waived. *For additional information:* Coordinator, Minority Affairs. Applications for aid are available after acceptance.

* member AMCAS

Loyola University of Chicago*
Stritch School of Medicine
2160 South First Avenue
Maywood, IL 60153

NEW MCAT: required

GPA: 3.5 overall

FOUNDED 1915; *private.*

ENROLLMENT: 320 men, 190 women (total); 85 men, 50 women (first-year).

COSTS: tuition $12,800 ($16,300 out-of-state), student fees $650, other expenses $8200.

APPLICATIONS should be submitted between June 15 and November 15; the application fee is $35. Notification begins October 15; response must be received within 2 weeks; no deposit is needed to hold place in class. Early Decision plan is available. Some preference is given to state residents and to applicants committed to the needs of the Illinois health care system. Admission factors weighted most heavily are the New MCAT, GPA, character, evidence of community service and motivation. *Correspondence to:* Office of Admissions, Room 1752.

MINORITY STUDENTS comprise 4% of the total student body, 4% of the first-year class. The $35 application fee may be waived. *For additional information:* Dr. Michael Rainey, Associate Dean for Student Affairs. Applications for aid should be made upon acceptance.

* member AMCAS

Marshall University*
School of Medicine
1542 Spring Valley Drive
Huntington, WV 25704

NEW MCAT: required

GPA: 3.5 overall

FOUNDED 1972; *publicly controlled.*

ENROLLMENT: 120 men, 75 women (total); 30 men, 20 women (first-year).

COSTS: tuition $3250 ($6250 out-of-state), student fees $300, other expenses $7600.

APPLICATIONS should be submitted between June 15 and November 15; the application fee is $20. Notification begins October 15; response must be received within 2 weeks of notification; no deposit needed to hold place in class. Preference is given to state residents. Selection factors include academic records, MCAT scores, and personal qualifications. *Correspondence to:* Admissions Office.

MINORITY STUDENTS comprise 2% of the total student body, 2% of the first-year class. *For additional information:* Associate Dean for Student Affairs.

* member AMCAS

Mayo Medical School*
200 First Street, S.W.
Rochester, MN 55905

NEW MCAT: required

GPA: 3.7 overall, 3.7 science

FOUNDED 1971; *private,* academic affiliation with University of Minnesota, associated with the Mayo Clinic.

ENROLLMENT: 90 men, 65 women (total); 25 men, 15 women (first-year).

COSTS: tuition $7100 ($15,000 out-of-state), student fees $750, other expenses $7900.

APPLICATIONS should be submitted between June 15 and November 15; the application fee is $40. Notification begins October 15; response must be received within 2 weeks; $100 deposit required to hold place in class. Early Decision plan is available. Slight preference is given to state residents; 20 places in the first-year class are reserved for nonresidents. Admission factors counted most heavily include GPA, New MCAT, interviews and letters of recommendation. *Correspondence to:* Admissions Committee.

MINORITY STUDENTS comprise 7% of the total student body, 5% of the first-year class. The medical school offers preadmission laboratory experiences, and tutoring programs for students of disadvantaged backgrounds. *For additional information:* Admissions Office. Application for aid should be made upon acceptance.

* member AMCAS

Medical College of Georgia*
School of Medicine
1120 Fifteenth Street
Augusta, GA 30912

NEW MCAT: required

GPA: 3.5 overall, 3.5 science

FOUNDED 1828; *publicly controlled*; a unit of the Georgia
   University System. Optional three-year degree granting
   program available.

ENROLLMENT: 540 men, 190 women (total), 130 men, 60
   women (first-year).

COSTS: tuition $2500 ($7500 out-of-state), student fees
   $200, other expenses $8200.

APPLICATIONS should be submitted between June 15 and
   November 1; there is no application fee. Notification
   begins October 15; response must be received within 3
   weeks; $50 deposit required to hold place in class. Early
   Decision plan is available for Georgia residents only.
   Preference is given to state residents; a maximum of 5%
   of the first-year places is open to nonresidents. Admission factors include academic aptitude and performance,
   New MCAT scores, potential to practice medicine as
   evaluated by premedical advisor, personal references,
   and the personal interview. *Correspondence to:* Associate Dean for Admissions.

MINORITY STUDENTS comprise 7% of the total student body,
   9% of the first-year class; most of these students are receiving aid. The School of Medicine sponsors a summer
   program for premedical minority students as part of its
   recruitment program for such students. *For additional
   information:* Assistant Professor, Medical Education
   and Minority Affairs.

* member AMCAS

Medical College of Ohio*
Caller Service No. 10008
Toledo, OH 43699

NEW MCAT: required

GPA: 3.5 overall, 3.2 science

FOUNDED 1964; *publicly controlled.*

ENROLLMENT: 360 men, 180 women (total); 100 men, 55 women (first-year).

COSTS: tuition $6400 ($8750 out-of-state), student fees $250, other expenses $8600.

APPLICATIONS should be submitted between June 15 and December 1; the application fee is $30. Notification begins October 15; response must be received by school within two weeks; no deposit needed to hold place in class. Early Decision plan is available. Preference is given to state residents. *Correspondence to:* Admissions Office.

MINORITY STUDENTS comprise 6% of the total student body, 9% of the first-year class. *For additional information:* Dr. Barry Richardson, Associate Dean of Minority Affairs.

153

Medical College of Pennsylvania*
3300 Henry Avenue
Philadelphia, PA 19129

NEW MCAT: required

GPA: 3.5 overall, 3.5 science

FOUNDED 1850; *private*. Combined baccalaureate-M.D. program available for high school graduates; special arrangements with Lehigh University and Bryn Mawr College.

ENROLLMENT: 190 men, 280 women (total); 45 men, 70 women (first-year).

COSTS: tuition $13,950, student fees $1150, other expenses $9500.

APPLICATIONS should be submitted between June 15 and December 1; the application fee is $55. Notification begins October 15; response must be received within 2 weeks; $100 deposit needed to hold place in class. Early Decision plan is available. Preference is given to state residents. Admission criteria include evidence of intellectual excellence, integrity, emotional maturity, motivation, as well as GPA and New MCAT scores. *Correspondence to:* Associate Dean for Student Affairs (Admissions).

MINORITY STUDENTS comprise 8% of the total student enrollment, 9% of the first-year class; most of these students receive aid. The $40 application fee (upon request) may be waived. As a participant in the Philadelphia Center for Health Careers, the Medical College recruits and counsels disadvantaged students in attaining health service careers. The Center gives particular attention to residents of Pennsylvania and the Greater Delaware Valley Area. *For additional information:* Associate Dean and Director, Minority Affairs. Upon acceptance, students may apply for aid.

* member AMCAS

Medical College of Wisconsin*
8701 Watertown Plank Road
Milwaukee, WI 53226

NEW MCAT: required

GPA: 3.7 overall, 3.7 science

FOUNDED 1913; *private, with state support.*

ENROLLMENT: 530 men, 250 women (total); 135 men, 70 women (first-year).

COSTS: tuition $7700 ($17,600 out-of-state), student fees $800, other expenses $9100.

APPLICATIONS should be submitted between June 15 and December 1; the application fee is $45. Notification begins November 1; response must be received within 3 weeks; $100 deposit needed to hold place in class. Early Decision plan is available. Preference given to state residents; more than half of recent entering classes have been from Wisconsin. Admission criteria include GPA, New MCAT, candidate's statement in application, academic recommendations, personal interview, and suitability for the medical profession. *Correspondence to:* Director of Admissions and Registrar.

MINORITY STUDENTS comprise 4% of the total student body, 5% of the first-year class. The $45 application fee may be waived. A subcommittee which includes minority group membership from the faculty recommends selected minority applicants to the Committee on Admissions. *For additional information:* Associate Dean for Academic Affairs. Students may apply for aid as soon as they have been accepted and indicate their intent to enroll.

* member AMCAS

Medical University of South Carolina*
College of Medicine
171 Ashley Avenue
Charleston, SC 29425

NEW MCAT: required

GPA: 3.5 overall

FOUNDED 1824; *publicly controlled.*

ENROLLMENT: 400 men, 200 women (total); 95 men, 50 women (first-year).

COSTS: tuition and fees $3900 ($7900 out-of-state), other expenses $10,400.

APPLICATIONS should be submitted between June 15 and December 1; the application fee is $15. Notification begins October 15, response must be received by school within 2 weeks; no deposit needed to hold place in class. Early Decision plan is available for South Carolina residents only. Strong preference is given to state residents. In recent years about 95% of first-year students have been state residents. Admission factors counted most heavily are the New MCAT, GPA, recommendations, and personal characteristics. *Correspondence to:* University Registrar and Director of Admissions.

MINORITY STUDENTS comprise 3% of the total student body, 5% of the first-year class. *For additional information:* Office of Minority Affairs.

* member AMCAS

Meharry Medical College*
School of Medicine
1005 D. B. Todd, Jr. Boulevard
Nashville, TN 37208

NEW MCAT: required

GPA: 3.1 overall, 3.1 science

FOUNDED 1876; *private*, with support from states participating in the Southern Regional Educational Board (AL,
FL, GA, LA, MD, MS, NC, TN, and VA).

ENROLLMENT: 170 men, 135 women (total); 50 men, 55
women (first-year).

COSTS: tuition $10,600, student fees $900, other expenses
$7400.

APPLICATIONS should be submitted between June 15 and
December 15; the application fee is $25. Notification
begins October 15; response must be received by school
within 3 weeks; $100 deposit needed to hold place in
class. Early Decision plan is available. Preference is
given to residents of states which are members of the
Southern Regional Educational Board. Admission factors weighted most heavily include GPA, New MCAT
scores, recommendations, and interest in primary health
care. *Correspondence to:* Director, Admissions and Records.

MINORITY STUDENTS comprise 80% of the student body, 80%
of the first-year class; most of these students receive aid;
most remain to graduate. The $25 application fee may
be waived. The School of Medicine sponsors recruiting
seminars and a Summer Bio-medical Science Program
for minority and disadvantaged students. Tutorial assistance is available during the academic year. *For additional information:* Associate Dean for Student Affairs. Application for aid should be made after
acceptance, prior to July 15.

* member AMCAS

Mercer University*
School of Medicine
1550 College Street
Macon, GA 31207

NEW MCAT: required

GPA: not available

FOUNDED 1972; *private*

ENROLLMENT: 70 men, 40 women (total); 30 men, 15 women (first-year).

COSTS: tuition $12,000, student fees $400, other expenses $9100.

APPLICATIONS should be submitted between June 15 and December 1; the application fee is $25. Notification begins October 15; response must be received within 2 weeks; $100 deposit needed to reserve place in class. Early Decision plan is available for Georgia residents only. Admission factors include academic and personal potential, letters of recommendation or premedical committee evaluation, and personal interview. *Correspondence to:* Office of Admissions and Student Affairs.

MINORITY STUDENTS comprise 6% of the total student body, 11% of the first-year class. *For additional information:* Associate Dean for Community Relations.

* member AMCAS

Michigan State University*
College of Human Medicine
East Lansing, MI 48824

NEW MCAT: required

GPA: not available

FOUNDED 1964; *publicly controlled.*

ENROLLMENT: 230 men, 220 women (total); 55 men, 50 women (first-year).

COSTS: tuition $4400 ($9500 out-of-state), student fees $350, other expenses $9000.

APPLICATIONS should be submitted between June 15 and December 1; the application fee is $20. Notification begins October 15; response must be received within 2 weeks; $50 deposit needed to reserve place in class. Early Decision plan is available. Preference given to state residents; approximately 90% of recent first-year students have been Michigan residents. Admission critgeria include academic performance and trends, New MCAT scores, letters of recommendation, relevant work experience, suitability for the MSU program, and the personal interview. *Correspondence to:* Office of Admissions, A-239 Life Sciences.

MINORITY STUDENTS comprise 18% of the total student body, 17% of the first-year class; about 90% of these students receive aid. The $20 application fee may be waived. *For additional information:* Director of Student Affairs.

* member AMCAS

Morehouse School of Medicine*
820 Westview Drive, S.W.
Atlanta, GA 30310

NEW MCAT: required

GPA: not available

FOUNDED 1978; *private*

ENROLLMENT: 70 men and 70 women (total); 20 men, 20 women (first-year).

COSTS: tuition $11,000, student fees $1200, other expenses $9600.

APPLICATIONS should be submitted between June 15 and December 1; the application fee is $100. Notification begins October 15; response must be received within 2 weeks; $100 deposit needed to hold place in class. Early Decision plan is available for minority applicants only. Admission factors are MCAT scores, undergraduate curriculum and record, extent and nature of extracurricular activities, and personal qualifications. Preference given to residents of Georgia, Alabama, and New York, but well-qualified nonresidents are encouraged to apply. Most students are black. *Correspondence to:* Admissions and Student Affairs.

MINORITY STUDENTS comprise 82% of the total student body, 80% of the first-year class. *For additional information:* Admissions and Student Affairs.

* member AMCAS

Mount Sinai School of Medicine*
of the City University of New York
1 Gustave L. Levy Place—Box 1002
New York, NY 10029

NEW MCAT: required

GPA: 3.6 overall

FOUNDED 1963; *private, affiliated with CUNY.*

ENROLLMENT: 285 men, 205 women (total); 65 men, 50 women (first-year).

COSTS: tuition $14,800, student fees, $750, other expenses $9900.

APPLICATIONS should be submitted between June 15 and November 1; the application fee is $50. Notification begins December 1; response must be received within 2 weeks; no deposit needed to hold place in class. Early Decision plan is available. *Correspondence to:* Assistant Dean for Admissions and Student Affairs, Room 5-04, Annenberg Building.

MINORITY STUDENTS comprise 8% of the total student body, 10% of the first-year class. The School of Medicine offers a preentrance summer program for accepted students in addition to tutorial assistance during the academic year. *For additional information:* Assistant Dean, Admissions and Student Affairs. Applications for aid should be made upon acceptance.

* member AMCAS

New York Medical College*
Elmwood Hall
Valhalla, NY 10595

NEW MCAT: required

GPA: 3.5 overall

FOUNDED 1860; *private.*

ENROLLMENT: 495 men, 265 women (total); 105 men, 75 women (first-year).

COSTS: tuition $21,000, student fees $250, other expenses $12,400.

APPLICATIONS should be submitted between June 15 and December 1; the application fee is $50. Notification begins October 15; response must be received within 2 weeks; $500 deposit needed to hold place in class. Early Decision plan is available. Admission factors include the New MCAT, GPA, a premedical curriculum, recommendations, motivation and integrity. *Correspondence to:* Office of Admissions, Room 127, Sunshine Cottage.

MINORITY STUDENTS comprise 9% of the total student body; 15% of the first-year students. Financial assistance is available; more than half of the students receive aid. The $50 application fee may be waived. *For additional information:* Dr. Anthony A. Clemendor, Associate Dean for Minority Affairs. Applications for aid should be made as early as possible.

* member AMCAS

New York University
School of Medicine
550 First Avenue
New York City, NY 10016

NEW MCAT: required

GPA: not available

FOUNDED 1841; *private.*

ENROLLMENT: 405 men, 215 women (total); 90 men, 60
women (first-year).

COSTS: tuition and student fees $15,880, other expenses
$12,400.

APPLICATIONS should be submitted between August 15 and
December 15; the application fee is $50. Notification
begins December 15; response must be received within
2 weeks; $100 deposit needed to secure position in the
class. Selection criteria include academic performance,
New MCAT results, letters of recommendation, the personal interview, aptitude, and motivation. *Correspondence to:* Office of Admissions.

MINORITY STUDENTS comprise 2% of the student body, 1%
of the first-year class; most of these students are receiving aid. The $35 application fee may be waived. *For
additional information:* Dr. Veva Zimmerman, Associate Dean, Student Affairs. Accepted students are eligible
to file applications for financial assistance.

Northeastern Ohio Universities*
College of Medicine
4209 State Route 44
P.O. Box 95
Rootstown, OH 44272

NEW MCAT: required

GPA: 3.4 overall

FOUNDED 1973; *publicly supported.* Special programs include a combined B.S.-M.D. program for high school graduates.

ENROLLMENT: 250 men, 145 women (total); 55 men, 45 women (first-year).

COSTS: tuition $5500 ($11,000 out-of-state), student fees $950, other expenses $6900.

APPLICATIONS should be submitted between June 15 and November 1; the application fee is $20. Notification begins October 15; response must be received within 2 weeks; no deposit needed to hold place in class. Early Decision plan is available. Preference is given to state residents. Selection factors include academic records, MCAT scores, personal qualifications, and demonstration of sincere motivation for the practice of medicine. *Correspondence to:* Office of Student Affairs.

MINORITY STUDENTS comprise 2% of the total student body, 1% of the first-year class. *For additional information:* Director of Minority Affairs.

* member AMCAS

Northwestern University*
Medical School
303 East Chicago Avenue
Chicago, IL 60611

NEW MCAT: required

GPA: 3.6 overall

FOUNDED 1859; *private, with state support.* Special programs include an Honors Program in Medical Education leading to the M.D. degree after 3 years of undergraduate work at the Evanston campus and 4 years at Northwestern; and a 7-year program leading to the B.S. degree in engineering and an M.D. degree.

ENROLLMENT: 400 men, 270 women (total); 105 men, 70 women (first-year). 60 members of each class are admitted from the Honors Programs.

COSTS: tuition $17,500, student fees $350, other expenses $8100.

APPLICATIONS should be submitted between June 15 and November 15; the application fee is $50. Notification begins October 1; response must be received within 2 weeks; no deposit is necessary to hold a place in class. Early Decision plan is available. Preference is given to state residents; one-half of students admitted must be Illinois residents, inclusive of the Honors program. Admission factors include academic performance, personal qualifications and achievements, and a personal interview. *Correspondence to:* Northwestern University Medical School.

MINORITY STUDENTS comprise 3% of the student body, 5% of the first-year class. *For additional information:* Associate Dean, Educational Programs. Applications for aid may be submitted only upon acceptance to the school; deadline July 1.

* member AMCAS

Ohio State University*
College of Medicine
370 West Ninth Avenue
Columbus, OH 43210

NEW MCAT: required

GPA: 3.5 overall, 3.5 science

FOUNDED 1914; *publicly controlled.* The Independent Study Program provides the option to complete the M.D. degree requirements within three calendar years.

ENROLLMENT: 605 men, 330 women (total); 160 men, 90 women (first-year).

COSTS: tuition and fees $3200 ($9100 out-of-state), other expenses $6100.

APPLICATIONS should be submitted between June 15 and November 15; the application fee is $10. Notification begins October 15; response must be received within two weeks; no deposit needed to hold place in class. Early Decision plan is available. Preference is given to state residents. Admission criteria include GPA, New MCAT, letters of recommendation, the personal interview, and nonacademic achievements. *Correspondence to:* Admissions Committee, 270-A, Meiling Hall.

MINORITY STUDENTS comprise 5% of the total enrollment and 9% of the first-year class. Academic assistance programs are available to students who exhibit special academic needs. *For additional information:* Special Assistant for Student Affairs.

* member AMCAS

166

Oral Roberts University*
School of Medicine
8181 South Lewis Avenue
Tulsa, OK 74137

NEW MCAT: required

GPA: 3.5 overall, 3.5 science

FOUNDED 1979; *private*

ENROLLMENT: 140 men, 40 women (total); 40 men, 10 women (first-year).

COSTS: tuition $15,000, student fees $150, other expenses $7400.

APPLICATIONS should be submitted between June 15 and December 15; the application fee is $35. Notification begins October 15; response must be received by school within 1 month; $100 deposit needed to hold place in class. Early Decision plan is available. Selection factors include academic records, MCAT scores, letters of recommendation, and personal interviews. *Correspondence to:* Office of Admissions.

MINORITY STUDENTS comprise 4% of the total student body, 4% of the first-year students. The $35 application fee may be waived. The school seeks qualified applicants from minority groups underrepresented in medicine. *For additional information:* Assistant Dean for Student Affairs.

* member AMCAS

Oregon Health Sciences University*†
School of Medicine
3181 S.W. Sam Jackson Park Road
Portland, OR 97201

NEW MCAT: required

GPA: 3.6 overall

FOUNDED 1887; *publicly controlled.*

ENROLLMENT: 245 men, 125 women (total); 60 men, 35 women (first-year).

COSTS: tuition $4400 ($9400 out-of-state), student fees $650, other expenses $6100.

APPLICATIONS should be submitted between June 15 and November 15; the application fee is $25. Notification begins December 1; response must be received by school within two weeks; no deposit needed to hold place in class. Preference is given to state residents and residents of neighboring western states without medical schools (Alaska, Idaho, Montana, Wyoming). Admission factors include preprofessional training, evidence of scholarship, New MCAT scores, evaluations from pre-medical instructors, evidence of good moral character, and the personal interview. *Correspondence to:* Director of Admissions.

MINORITY STUDENTS comprise 1–2% of the study body. *For additional information:* Associate Director, Office of Minority Student Affairs. Applications for aid should be submitted upon acceptance, prior to March 1.

* member AMCAS
†member WICHE

Pennsylvania State University*
College of Medicine
500 University Drive
Hershey, PA 17033

NEW MCAT: required

GPA: 3.6 overall

FOUNDED 1964; *publicly controlled.*

ENROLLMENT: 225 men, 120 women (total); 55 men, 35 women (first-year).

COSTS: tuition $10,500 ($16,500 out-of-state), student fees $400, other expenses $9300.

APPLICATIONS should be submitted between June 15 and November 15; the application fee is $40. Notification begins October 15; response must be received by school within 2 weeks; $100 deposit needed to hold place in class. Early Decision plan is available. Preference is given to state residents. Selection factors include GPA, New MCAT, letters of recommendation, and an interview. *Correspondence to:* Office of Student Affairs.

MINORITY STUDENTS comprise 5% of the total student body, 2% of first-year students; most of these students receive aid. The College of Medicine has organized a special recruitment program for minorities and students from disadvantaged backgrounds. *For additional information:* Dr. Alphonse E. LeuredePree, Assistant Dean for Student Affairs.

* member AMCAS

Ponce School of Medicine*
P.O. Box 7004
Ponce, PR 00732

NEW MCAT: required

GPA: 3.4 overall

FOUNDED 1980 (originally Catholic University of Puerto Rico School of Medicine); *private.*

ENROLLMENT: 105 men, 65 women (total); 30 men, 20 women (first-year).

COSTS: tuition $13,500 ($20,500 out-of-state), student fees $500, other expenses $11,000.

APPLICATIONS should be submitted between June 15 and December 15; the application fee is $50. Notification begins December 1; response must be received within 3 weeks; $1000 deposit is necessary to hold place in class. Early Decision plan is available for Puerto Rico residents only. Admission decisions are based on the MCAT score, GPA, recommendations, and personal interview. Preference is given to residents of Puerto Rico; since courses are taught in both English and Spanish, students must have functional knowledge of both languages. *Correspondence to:* Admissions Office.

* member AMCAS

Rush Medical College of Rush University*
600 South Paulina Street
Chicago, IL 60612

NEW MCAT: required

GPA: not available

FOUNDED 1837, closed 1942 and reopened in 1971; *private.*

ENROLLMENT: 300 men, 195 women (total); 65 men, 55 women (first-year).

COSTS: tuition $15,000, student fees $400, other expenses $8200.

APPLICATIONS should be submitted between June 15 and November 15; the application fee is $35. Notification begins October 15; response must be received within 2 weeks; $100 deposit is needed to hold place in class. Early Decision plan is available. Strong preference is given to state residents. Admission criteria include academic performance, New MCAT results, letters of recommendation, and the personal interview. *Correspondence to:* Office of Admissions.

MINORITY STUDENTS comprise 6% of the total student enrollment, 9% of the first-year class; most of these students receive aid. The $35 application fee may be waived. *For additional information:* Chairperson, Committee on Admissions. Applications for aid may be made upon acceptance.

* member AMCAS

Saint Louis University*
School of Medicine
1402 South Grand Boulevard
St. Louis, MO 63104

NEW MCAT: required

GPA: 3.6 overall, 3.6 science

FOUNDED 1836; *private.*

ENROLLMENT: 465 men, 140 women (total): 125 men, 35 women (first-year).

COSTS: tuition $16,500, other expenses $8200.

APPLICATIONS should be submitted between June 15 and December 15; the application fee is $45. Notification begins October 15; response must be received within 2 weeks; $100 deposit needed to hold place in class. Early Decision plan is available. Admissions qualifications include the New MCAT, GPA, demonstrated scientific ability, character, and motivation. *Correspondence to:* Admissions Committee.

MINORITY STUDENTS comprise less than 1% of the total student body; most of these students receive aid. The $45 application fee may be waived. *For additional information:* Associate Dean, Admissions and Student Affairs.

* member AMCAS

Southern Illinois University*
School of Medicine
P.O. Box 19230
Springfield, IL 62794

NEW MCAT: required

GPA: 3.5 overall, 3.5 science

FOUNDED 1969; *publicly controlled.*

ENROLLMENT: 190 men, 85 women (total); 45 men, 25 women (first-year).

COSTS: tuition $4800, student fees $750, other expenses $8700.

APPLICATIONS should be submitted between June 15 and November 15; there is no application fee. Notification begins October 15; response must be received within 2 weeks; $100 deposit required to hold place in class. Early Decision plan is available. Acceptances are offered only to state residents. Admission requirements include GPA, New MCAT, interviews, and letters of academic recommendation. *Correspondence to:* Office of the Dean of Students.

MINORITY STUDENTS comprise 11% of the total student body, 9% of the first-year class. The School of Medicine sponsors a Medical Education Preparatory Program (MED-PREP) to aid minority students in preparing for medical school. *For additional information:* Assistant Dean of Student/Admissions.

* member AMCAS

Stanford University*†
School of Medicine
851 Welch Road
Palo Alto, CA 94304

NEW MCAT: required

GPA: 3.6 overall

FOUNDED 1908; *private*; a flexible curriculum allows completion of the M.D. program in three to five years.

ENROLLMENT: 310 men, 135 women (total); 55 men, 35 women (first-year).

COSTS: tuition $17,000, other expenses $9100.

APPLICATIONS should be submitted between June 15 and November 1; the application fee is $55. Notification begins October 15; response must be received within 3 weeks; no deposit needed to hold place in class. Early Decision plan is available. Selection factors include academic record and demonstrated motivational and personal qualifications for medicine. *Correspondence to:* Office of Admissions, Room 154.

MINORITY STUDENTS comprise 17% of total enrollment, 15% of the first-year class; most of these students receive aid. The School of Medicine has a strong commitment to recruit women and minority students, particularly blacks, Mexican-Americans, and American Indians. *For additional information:* Assistant Dean for Student Affairs. Applications for aid are available after acceptance.

* member AMCAS
† member WICHE

174

State University of New York*
Health Science Center at Brooklyn
College of Medicine
450 Clarkson Avenue
Brooklyn, NY 11203

NEW MCAT: required

GPA: 3.6 overall, 3.4 science

FOUNDED 1860 (acquired by state system in 1950); *publicly controlled.*

ENROLLMENT: 580 men, 300 women (total); 140 men, 85 women (first-year).

COSTS: tuition $5600 ($8900 out-of-state), student fees $150, other expenses $5600.

APPLICATIONS should be submitted between June 15 and December 15; the application fee is $50. Notification begins October 15; response must be received within 2 weeks; no deposit needed to hold place in class. Strong preference given to state residents. Admissions decisions are based on college records, letters of recommendation, New MCAT scores, the interview, and health records. *Correspondence to:* Associate Dean/Chairman of Admissions.

MINORITY STUDENTS comprise 11% of the total student body, 12% of first-year students. Various scholarships, work-study programs and loans are available; most students receive assistance. *For additional information:* Associate Dean and Deputy Assistant Vice President.

* member AMCAS

State University of New York*
Health Science Center at Syracuse
College of Medicine
155 Elizabeth Blackwell Street
Syracuse, NY 13210

NEW MCAT: required

GPA: 3.5 overall

FOUNDED 1834 (acquired by state system in 1950); *publicly controlled.*

ENROLLMENT: 390 men, 225 women (total); 105 men, 55 women (first-year).

COSTS: tuition $5600 ($8900 out-of-state), student fees $100, other expenses $7000.

APPLICATIONS should be submitted between June 15 and December 1; the application fee is $50. Notification begins October 15; response must be received within 14 days; no deposit needed to hold place in class. Early Decision plan is available. Strong preference given to state residents; over 95% of a recent first-year class was from New York. Admission factors include scholastic and scientific aptitude and performance, New MCAT scores, letters of recommendation, personal qualifications, and the personal interview. *Correspondence to:* Admissions Committee.

MINORITY STUDENTS comprise 8% of the total enrollment, 12% of the first-year class; most of these students receive aid. The College of Medicine sponsors the Upstate-Minority Educational Development Program to support the academic needs of students of disadvantaged backgrounds. *For additional information:* Dr. Norton Berg, Assistant Dean for Academic Achievement. Application for aid should be made upon acceptance.

* member AMCAS

State University of New York at Buffalo*
School of Medicine and Biomedical Sciences
3435 Main Street
Buffalo, NY 14214

NEW MCAT: required

GPA: 3.4 overall (minimum)

FOUNDED 1846 (acquired by state system in 1962); *publicly controlled.* Optional three-year program available.

ENROLLMENT: 345 men, 225 women (total); 85 men, 60 women (first-year).

COSTS: tuition $5600 ($8900 out-of-state), student fees $300, other expenses $9500.

APPLICATIONS should be submitted between June 15 and December 1; the application fee is $50. Notification begins October 15, response must be received within 2 weeks; $100 deposit needed to hold place in class. Strong preference given to state residents. Admission factors weighted most heavily include GPA, New MCAT, letters of recommendation, and the personal interview. Candidates should also demonstrate such personal qualifications as a habit of critical analysis, a spirit of inquiry, and a sense of understanding and sympathy for those who suffer. While admission decisions are based on merit, the percentage of women enrolled has traditionally been greater than the percentage of women in the applicant pool. *Correspondence to:* Office of Medical Admissions, Farber Hall.

MINORITY STUDENTS comprise 15% of the total student enrollment, 16% of the first-year class. The $50 application fee may be waived. The School of Medicine sponsors a special summer program for minority and disadvantaged students. Remedial sessions are provided for all students during the academic year. *For additional information:* Assistant Dean and Director, Minority Affairs. Applications for aid are provided upon acceptance.

* member AMCAS

State University of New York at Stony Brook*
Health Sciences Center
School of Medicine
Stony Brook, NY 11794

NEW MCAT: required

GPA: not available

FOUNDED 1971; *publicly controlled.*

ENROLLMENT: 275 men, 170 women (total); 65 men, 50 women (first-year).

COSTS: tuition $5600 ($8600 out-of-state), student fees $75, other expenses $11,100.

APPLICATIONS should be submitted between June 15 and December 15; the application fee is $50. Notification begins in September; response must be received within 14 days; no deposit needed to reserve place in class. Early Decision plan is available. Strong preference given to state residents; approximately 95% of recent entrants are from New York state. Admission decisions are based on New MCAT, GPA, recommendation of pre-medical advisor, and excellent personal abilities. *Correspondence to:* Committee on Admissions.

MINORITY STUDENTS comprise 6% of the total student body, 10% of first-year students. Students may avail themselves of a variety of state, federal, and private programs of financial assistance which are administered by the Office of Student Services. *For additional information:* Dr. Aldustus E. Jordan, Associate Dean.

* member AMCAS

Temple University*
School of Medicine
3400 North Broad Street
Philadelphia, PA 19140

NEW MCAT: required

GPA: 3.3 overall

FOUNDED 1901; *state-related.*

ENROLLMENT: 480 men, 235 women (total); 130 men, 60 women (first-year).

COSTS: tuition $12,000 ($15,800 out-of-state), student fees $1050, other expenses $7500.

APPLICATIONS should be submitted between June 15 and December 1; the application fee is $40. Notification begins October 15; response must be received by school within two weeks; $100 deposit needed to hold place in class. Early Decision plan is available. Preference is given to state residents; about 25% may come from other states. Selection factors include academic performance, extracurricular activities, New MCAT scores, recommendations, and the interview. *Correspondence to:* Admissions Officer.

MINORITY STUDENTS comprise 15% of the total student body, 18% of the first-year class; most of these students receive aid. The $40 application fee may be waived. The School of Medicine operates the Recruitment, Admissions, and Retention (RAR) Program which actively identifies potential minority applicants and provides special follow-up services and financial aid during the term of their medical education. Matriculation summer program is offered for accepted minority students. *For additional information:* Charles S. Ireland, Jr., Assistant to the Dean.

* member AMCAS

Texas A & M University
College of Medicine
College Station, TX 77843

NEW MCAT: required

GPA: 3.5 overall

FOUNDED 1971, admitted first class in 1977; *publicly controlled.*

ENROLLMENT: 120 men, 75 women (total); 30 men, 25 women (first-year).

COSTS: tuition $4500 ($18,000 out-of-state), student fees $750, other expenses $9100.

APPLICATIONS should be submitted between May 3 and November 1; the application fee is $35. Notification begins November 15; response must be received within 2 weeks; no deposit needed to hold place in class. Preference is given to state residents. Admission factors include academic records, MCAT scores, personal qualifications, and demonstration of motivation. *Correspondence to:* Associate Dean for Student Affairs.

MINORITY STUDENTS comprise 10% of the total student body, 11% of the first-year class. *For additional information:* Associan Dean for Admissions and Student Affairs.

180

Texas Tech University
Health Sciences Center
School of Medicine
Fourth Street and Indiana Avenue
Lubbock, TX 79430

NEW MCAT: required

GPA: 3.4 overall

FOUNDED 1969; *publicly controlled.*

ENROLLMENT: 280 men, 125 women (total); 85 men, 25 women (first-year).

COSTS: tuition $4400, student fees $450, other expenses $10,300.

APPLICATIONS should be submitted between June 15 and November 1; the application fee is $30. Notification begins October 15; response must be received by school within 2 weeks; $100 deposit needed to hold place in class. Early Decision plan is available. Strong preference is given to state residents; in recent years almost all entrants have been Texans. Admissions decisions are based on New MCAT, GPA, breadth and strength of undergraduate curriculum, letters of recommendation, and the personal interview. *Correspondence to:* Office of Admissions.

MINORITY STUDENTS comprise 6% of the total student body, 5% of first-year students. Upon acceptance students may apply for aid. *For additional information:* Associate Dean for Admissions and Student Affairs.

Tufts University*
School of Medicine
136 Harrison Avenue
Boston, MA 02111

NEW MCAT: required

GPA: 3.0 overall (minimum)

FOUNDED 1852; *private.*

ENROLLMENT: 390 men, 210 women (total); 90 men, 65 women (first-year).

COSTS: tuition and fees $19,500, other expenses $9300.

APPLICATIONS should be submitted between June 15 and November 1; the application fee is $55. Notification begins October 15; response must be received within 2 weeks of notification; $100 deposit needed to hold place in class. Early Decision plan is available. Admission factors counted most heavily include GPA, New MCAT, caliber of college work, personality, and motivation. *Correspondence to:* Committee on Admissions.

MINORITY STUDENTS comprise 8% of the student body, 10% of the first-year class. The $55 application fee (on request) may be waived. *For additional information:* Coordinator, Minority Affairs Office. Applications for aid are available upon acceptance.

* member AMCAS

Tulane University*
School of Medicine
1430 Tulane Avenue
New Orleans, LA 70112

NEW MCAT: required

GPA: 3.5 overall, 3.5 science

FOUNDED 1834; *private.*

ENROLLMENT: 410 men, 200 women (total); 110 men, 45 women (first-year).

COSTS: tuition and fees $20,000, other expenses $9600.

APPLICATIONS should be submitted between June 15 and December 15; the application fee is $55. Notification begins October 15; response must be received within 2 weeks; $100 deposit required to hold place in class. Admission factors weighted most heavily include GPA (overall and science), New MCAT scores, faculty recommendations, special accomplishments and talents, substance of undergraduate programs, and trends in academic performance. *Correspondence to:* Director of Admissions.

MINORITY STUDENTS comprise 7% of the total enrollment, 6% of the first-year students; a majority of these students receive aid. A prematriculation summer enrichment program is available to entering minority and other disadvantaged students, as well as tutorial and counseling services. *For additional information:* Dr. Anna Cherrie Epps, Assistant Dean for Student Services.

* member AMCAS

Uniformed Services University of the Health Sciences*
F. Edward Hébert School of Medicine
4301 Jones Bridge Road
Bethesda, MD 20814

NEW MCAT: required

GPA: 3.4 overall, 3.4 science

FOUNDED 1972; *publicly controlled.* The school aims to prepare men and women for careers as medical corps officers.

ENROLLMENT: 525 men, 120 women (total); 135 men, 25 women (first-year).

COSTS: There are no tuition charges, and books and supplies are also furnished without charge.

APPLICATIONS should be submitted between June 15 and November 1; there is no application fee. Notification begins November 1; response must be received within two weeks; no deposit required to hold place in class. Selection factors include letters of reference, personal statement, and a service preference statement. Transcripts should not be submitted until requested. *Correspondence to:* Admissions Office, Room A-1041.

MINORITY STUDENTS comprise 4% of the total study body, 6% of first-year students. The School of Medicine operates the Accession of Qualified Underrepresented Applicants (AQUA) program to increase the number of qualified minority and women applicants. *For additional information:* Director of Admissions/Registrar.

* member AMCAS

184

Universidad Central del Caribe*
School of Medicine
P.O. Box 935
Cayey, PR 00633

NEW MCAT: required

GPA: 3.1 overall

FOUNDED 1976; *private*

ENROLLMENT: 210 men, 105 women (total); 40 men, 25 women (first-year).

COSTS: tuition $13,000 ($20,000 nonresident); student fees $100, other expenses $7600.

APPLICATIONS should be submitted between June 15 and December 15; the application fee is $50. Notification begins October 15; response must be received within 3 weeks. $100 deposit needed to hold place in class. Early Decision plan is available for Puerto Rico residents only. Admission factors include undergraduate academic record, GPA, MCAT, personal interview, and letters of recommendation. *Correspondence to:* Office of Admissions.

* member AMCAS

University of Alabama*
School of Medicine
University Station
Birmingham, AL 35294

NEW MCAT: required

GPA: 3.4 overall, 3.4 science

FOUNDED 1859; *publicly controlled.*

ENROLLMENT: 465 men, 165 women (total); 110 men, 50 women (first-year).

COSTS: tuition $3950 ($12,610 out-of-state), student fees $1400, other expenses $8300.

APPLICATIONS should be submitted between June 15 and November 15; the application fee is $25. Notification begins October 15; response must be received within 2 weeks; $50 deposit needed to hold place in class. Early Decision plan is available for Alabama residents only. Preference is given to state residents. Admission factors weighted most heavily include GPA, New MCAT scores, letters of recommendation, the personal interview, and personal qualifications. *Correspondence to:* Director of Admissions.

MINORITY STUDENTS comprise 6% of the student body, 7% of the first-year class; most of these students are receiving aid. The $25 application fee may be waived. The Office of Minority Student Affairs and the Admissions Committee provide counsel to minority students interested in the study of medicine. *For additional information:* Medical Director. Applications for aid should be made by March 1.

* member AMCAS

University of Arizona*†
College of Medicine
Tucson, AZ 85724

NEW MCAT: required

GPA: 3.6 overall

FOUNDED 1967; *publicly controlled.*

ENROLLMENT: 205 men, 155 women (total); 45 men, 45 women (first-year).

COSTS: tuition $4900, other expenses $8300.

APPLICATIONS should be submitted between June 15 and November 1; there is no application fee. Notification begins January 15; response must be received within 2 weeks; no deposit needed to hold place in class. Only residents of Arizona and WICHE-certified residents of Idaho, Alaska, Montana, or Wyoming are considered for admission. Admissions decisions are based on the New MCAT, GPA, letters of recommendation, personal interview, character, and motivation. *Correspondence to:* Admissions Office.

MINORITY STUDENTS comprise 12% of the total student body, 15% of the first-year class. Various types of financial assistance are available to students. *For additional information:* Dr. Andrew M. Goldner, Associate Dean for Student Affairs. Application for aid may be made after acceptance.

* member AMCAS
†member WICHE

University of Arkansas*
College of Medicine
4301 West Markham Street
Little Rock, AR 72205

NEW MCAT: required

GPA: 3.4 overall

FOUNDED 1879; *publicly controlled.*

ENROLLMENT: 375 men, 160 women (total); 105 men, 45 women (first-year).

COSTS: tuition $5100 ($10,280 out-of-state), student fees $400, other expenses $6100.

APPLICATIONS should be submitted between June 15 and November 15; the application fee is $10. Notification begins December 15; response must be received within 2 weeks; no deposit required to hold place in class. Preference is given to state residents. Admission factors counted most heavily include GPA, New MCAT, premedical advisory committee and faculty evaluation, and medical faculty interview. *Correspondence to:* Office of Student Admissions, Slot 551.

MINORITY STUDENTS comprise 9% of the total student body, 11% of the first-year class. For *additional information:* Assistant Dean for Minority Student Affairs. Application for aid should be made after acceptance and prior to matriculation.

* member AMCAS

188

University of California, Davis*†
School of Medicine
Davis, CA 95616

NEW MCAT: required

GPA: 3.0 overall (minimum)

FOUNDED 1963, admitted first class in 1968; *publicly controlled.*

ENROLLMENT: 225 men, 160 women (total); 60 men, 40 women (first-year).

COSTS: tuition and fees $1650 ($5250 out-of-state), other expenses $7800.

APPLICATIONS should be submitted between June 15 and November 1; the application fee is $35. Notification begins October 15; response must be received within 2 weeks; no deposit required to secure place in class. Preference is given to state residents; over 95% of a recent first-year class were California residents. Admission factors include academic record, New MCAT results, and motivation and personal qualifications as judged from letters of recommendation and personal interview. *Correspondence to:* Chair, Admissions Committee.

MINORITY STUDENTS comprise 16% of the total student enrollment, 15% of the first-year class. The $35 application fee may be waived. The School of Medicine sponsors special recruitment and orientation programs for students of disadvantaged social and educational backgrounds. *For additional information:* Director, Health Resources Development Program. Applications for aid may be made after acceptance.

* member AMCAS
†member WICHE

University of California, Irvine*†
College of Medicine
Irvine, CA 92717

NEW MCAT: required

GPA: 3.6 nonscience, 3.6 science

FOUNDED 1965; *publicly supported.*

ENROLLMENT: 245 men, 150 women (total); 60 men, 40 women (first-year).

COSTS: tuition and fees $1550 ($5100 out-of-state), other expenses $8200.

APPLICATIONS should be submitted between June 15 and November 1; the application fee is $35. Notification begins November 15; response must be received within 2 weeks; no deposit needed to hold place in class. Preference given to state residents; approximately 5% of each class are nonresidents. Admission factors include GPA, New MCAT, letters of recommendation, and a personal interview. *Correspondence to:* Office of Admissions, E112 Medical Sciences Building.

MINORITY STUDENTS comprise 16% of the total student body, 20% of first-year students. Tutorial assistance and counseling are available to students. The college provides financial aid in the form of scholarships, grants, and loans. The $35 application fee may be waived. *For additional information:* Assistant Dean, Office of Student and Curricular Affairs. Application for aid should be made after acceptance.

* member AMCAS
†member WICHE

University of California, Los Angeles*†
UCLA School of Medicine
Center for Health Sciences
Los Angeles, CA 90024

NEW MCAT: required

GPA: 3.6 nonscience, 3.6 science

FOUNDED 1951; *publicly supported.*

ENROLLMENT: 390 men, 215 women (total); 85 men, 55 women (first-year).

COSTS: tuition and fees $1500 ($5600 out-of-state), other expenses $10,100.

APPLICATIONS should be submitted between June 15 and November 1; application fee is $35. Notification begins January 15; response must be received within 2 weeks; no deposit needed to secure place in class. In recent years, approximately 85% of entering students have been state residents. Admission criteria include GPA, New MCAT results, evaluation of accomplishments and character in letters of recommendation, and the personal interview. *Correspondence to:* Office of Student Affairs.

MINORITY STUDENTS comprise 22% of the total student body, 25% of the first-year class; most of these students receive aid. The $35 application fee may be waived. A subcommittee of the Admissions Committee, which includes minority faculty and students, is responsible for the evaluation of all applications from minority and disadvantaged students. *For additional information:* Director, Office of Special Education. Applications for aid are forwarded to entering freshmen prior to May.

* member AMCAS
†member WICHE

University of California, San Diego*†
School of Medicine
La Jolla, CA 92093

NEW MCAT: required

GPA: 3.6 overall, 3.6 science

FOUNDED 1968; *publicly controlled.*

ENROLLMENT: 340 men, 160 women (total); 90 men, 35 women (first-year).

COSTS: tuition and fees $1600 ($4500 out-of-state), other expenses $8100.

APPLICATIONS should be submitted between June 15 and November 1; the application fee is $35. Notification begins October 15; response must be received within 2 weeks; no deposit required to hold place in class. Preference given to state residents. Admission factors most heavily weighted include GPA, New MCAT, letters of recommendation, personal interviews, and the nature of scholarly and extracurricular activities. *Correspondence to:* Office of Admissions, M-021, Medical Teaching Facility.

MINORITY STUDENTS comprise 17% of the total student body, 18% of the first-year class; most of these students receive aid. The $35 application fee may be waived. *For additional information:* Dr. Percy J. Russell, Assistant Dean. Application for aid may be filed only upon acceptance.

* member AMCAS
†member WICHE

University of California, San Francisco*†
School of Medicine
San Francisco, CA 94143

NEW MCAT: required

GPA: 3.7 overall, 3.6 science

FOUNDED 1864; *publicly controlled.*

ENROLLMENT: 370 men, 285 women (total); 80 men, 75 women (first-year).

COSTS: tuition and fees $1600 ($4400 out-of-state), other expenses $8200.

APPLICATIONS should be submitted between June 15 and November 1; the application fee is $35. Notification begins November 15; response must be received within 2 weeks; no deposit needed to secure place in class. Preference is given to state residents; approximately 80% of a recent first-year class were California residents. Admission factors include academic record, New MCAT scores, evidence of motivation towards medicine, and personal qualifications. *Correspondence to:* School of Medicine, Admissions, C-200, Box 0408.

MINORITY STUDENTS comprise 19% of the student body, 20% of the first-year class; most of these students receive aid. The $35 application fee may be waived. The Health Sciences Minority Program provides admission assistance, financial aid, a comprehensive orientation program, and other services for socioeconomically disadvantaged students. *For additional information:* Admissions Office. Application for aid should be made after acceptance.

* member AMCAS
†member WICHE

University of Chicago*
The Pritzker School of Medicine
5841 South Maryland Avenue
Chicago, IL 60637

NEW MCAT: required

GPA: 3.7 nonscience, 3.7 science

FOUNDED 1927; *private.*

ENROLLMENT: 320 men, 110 women (total); 70 men, 35 women (first-year).

COSTS: tuition $13,500, student fees $550, other expenses $7600.

APPLICATIONS should be submitted between June 15 and December 15; the application fee is $40. Notification begins October 15; response must be received within 4 weeks; $100 deposit needed to hold place in class. Early Decision plan is available. No preference given to state residents, though approximately 40% of recent entering classes have been from Illinois. Selection factors include scholastic record, New MCAT results, personal qualifications, as well as extracurricular activities. *Correspondence to:* Office of Dean of Students, Billings Hospital, Room G-115A.

MINORITY STUDENTS comprise 4% of enrolled students, 2% of the first-year class; most of these students are receiving aid. The $40 application fee may be waived. *For additional information:* Assistant Dean for Students. Applications for aid may be submitted upon acceptance, and prior to May 1.

* member AMCAS

University of Cincinnati*
College of Medicine
231 Bethesda Avenue
Cincinnati, OH 45267

NEW MCAT: required

GPA: 3.4 overall

FOUNDED 1819; *publicly controlled.*

ENROLLMENT: 440 men, 240 women (total); 90 men, 65 women (first-year).

COSTS: tuition $6500 ($12,300 out-of-state), student fees $550, other expenses $10,500.

APPLICATIONS should be submitted between June 15 and November 15; the application fee is $25. Notification begins October 15; response must be received by school within two weeks; no deposit needed to hold place in class. Early Decision plan is available. Preference is given to state residents. *Correspondence to:* Office of Student Affairs.

MINORITY STUDENTS comprise 6% of the student body, 8% the first-year class; most of these students receive aid. The $25 application fee may be waived. The College of Medicine maintains prematriculation and tutorial programs for students of disadvantaged backgrounds. *For additional information:* Assistant Dean for Admissions. Applications for aid should be made by May 31.

* member AMCAS

University of Colorado*†
School of Medicine
4200 East Ninth Avenue
Denver, CO 80262

NEW MCAT: required

GPA: 3.5 overall, 3.8 science

FOUNDED 1883; *publicly controlled.*

ENROLLMENT: 290 men, 230 women (total); 75 men, 55 women (first-year).

COSTS: tuition $7450 ($30,200 out-of-state), student fees $700, other expenses $7800.

APPLICATIONS should be submitted between June 15 and November 1; the application fee is $40. Notification begins October 15; response must be received within 2 weeks; $200 deposit needed to hold place in class. Early Decision plan available. Preference is given first to Colorado residents and then to residents of western states without medical schools—Wyoming, Montana, Idaho, Alaska. Admission factors counted most heavily include GPA, New MCAT, the interview, and references. The acceptance rates for male and female applicants have been identical within recent years. *Correspondence to:* Office of Admissions and Records.

MINORITY STUDENTS comprise 1% of enrolled students, 2% of the first-year class; most of these students are receiving aid. The $40 application fee may be waived. *For additional information:* Director of Financial Aid. Application for aid must be made within 2 weeks after receipt of acceptance letter.

* member AMCAS
†member WICHE

University of Connecticut*
School of Medicine
263 Farmington Avenue
Farmington, CT 06032

NEW MCAT: required

GPA: 3.5 overall

FOUNDED 1963; *publicly controlled.*

ENROLLMENT: 200 men, 155 women (total); 40 men, 45 women (first-year).

COSTS: tuition $4600 ($11,000 out-of-state), student fees $2000, other expenses $8600.

APPLICATIONS should be submitted between June 15 and December 15; the application fee is $50. Notification begins October 15; response must be received within 2 weeks; $100 deposit is required to hold a place in class. Early Decision plan is available. Preference given to state residents. Admission factors include GPA, New MCAT scores, undergraduate curriculum, extracurricular activities, and letters of recommendation. *Correspondence to:* Office of Admissions and Student Affairs.

MINORITY STUDENTS comprise 7% of the student body, 7% of the first-year class; most of these students receive aid. *For additional information:* Associate Dean, Minority Student Affairs.

* member AMCAS

University of Florida*
  College of Medicine
  J. Hillis Miller Health Center
  Gainesville, FL 32610

NEW MCAT: required

GPA: 3.5 overall

FOUNDED 1956; *publicly controlled.*

ENROLLMENT: 300 men, 155 women (total); 75 men, 40 women (first-year).

COSTS: tuition $4700 ($11,400 out-of-state), other expenses $8100.

APPLICATIONS should be submitted between June 15 and December 1; the application fee is $15. Notification begins October 15; response must be received within 2 weeks; no deposit needed to hold place in class. Preference is given to Florida residents; in recent years more than 90% of entrants have been Floridians. Admissions decisions are based on the New MCAT, GPA, personal interview, and character. *Correspondence to:* Chairman, Medical Selections Committee, Box J-216.

MINORITY STUDENTS comprise 7% of the total student enrollment; 6% of first-year students. Many types of financial assistance are available; students should apply upon enrollment. *For additional information:* Will Sanders, Office of Minority Affairs.

* member AMCAS

University of Hawaii*†
John A. Burns School of Medicine
1960 East-West Road
Honolulu, HI 96822

NEW MCAT: required

GPA: 3.2 overall (minimum)

FOUNDED 1965 as a two-year institution, introduced four-year program in 1973; *publicly controlled.*

ENROLLMENT: 165 men, 85 women (total); 40 men, 20 women (first-year).

COSTS: tuition $4400 ($14,500 out-of-state), fees $100, other expenses $8000.

APPLICATIONS should be submitted between June 15 and December 1; there is no application fee. Notification begins October 15; response must be received within 2 weeks; no deposit required to hold place in class. Early Decision plan is available. Preference given to state residents. Admission factors weighted most heavily include GPA, New MCAT, interview, and letters of recommendation. *Correspondence to:* Office of Student Affairs.

DIVERSE ETHNIC backgrounds are represented in the faculty and student body. Of the total enrollment, 76% are from minority groups. The School of Medicine sponsors two programs for students unable to enter directly into the normal medical program: a remedial program in the premedical sciences and a decelerated program permitting the student 3 years, with tutorial assistance, to complete the work normally completed in 2 years. These programs are designed primarily for, but are not limited to, persons of Hawaiian, part-Hawaiian, Filipino, Samoan and Micronesian ancestry. There is no application fee. *For additional information:* Associate Dean for Student Affairs. Application for aid may be made upon acceptance.

* member AMCAS
†member WICHE

University of Health Sciences*
The Chicago Medical School
333 Green Bay Road
North Chicago, IL 60064

NEW MCAT: required

GPA: 3.3 overall

FOUNDED 1912; *private.*

ENROLLMENT: 445 men, 190 women (total); 105 men, 55 women (first-year).

COSTS: tuition $20,500, student fees $600, other expenses $9400.

APPLICATIONS should be submitted between June 15 and December 15; the application fee is $55. Notification begins November 15; response must be received within 2 weeks; $100 deposit needed to reserve place in class. Early Decision plan is available. Admissions decisions are based on the New MCAT, GPA, recommendations, character, motivation, and a personal interview. *Correspondence to:* Office of Admissions.

MINORITY STUDENTS comprise 2% of the total student body, 2% of first-year students. The Medical School sponsors a special orientation program for minority students; tutorial assistance and counseling are also available. *For more information:* Dr. Theodore Booden, Associate Dean, Student Affairs. Financial aid is available; apply after notification of acceptance.

* member AMCAS

200

University of Illinois*
College of Medicine
1737 West Polk Street
Chicago, IL 60612

NEW MCAT: required

GPA: not available

FOUNDED 1867; *publicly controlled.* College of Medicine programs are offered in four cities: Chicago, Urbana-Champaign, Peoria, and Rockford.

ENROLLMENT: 895 men, 410 women (total); 215 men, 120 women (first-year).

COSTS: tuition $7200 ($20,500 out-of-state), student fees $1000, other expenses $10,900.

APPLICATIONS should be submitted between June 15 and December 1; the application fee is $20. Notification begins October 15; response must be received within 2 weeks; $100 deposit required to reserve place in class. Early Decision plan is available. Strong preference is given to state residents. Admission factors counted most heavily include GPA, New MCAT, letters of academic recommendation, and the personal statement in the AMCAS application. *Correspondence to:* Office of Admissions and Records.

MINORITY STUDENTS comprise 18% of the total student body, 24% of the first-year class; most of these students receive aid. Pre-admissions counseling is provided through the Medical Opportunities Office, and tutorial assistants are available to those students requiring additional instruction during the academic year. The $20 application fee may be waived. *For additional information:* Associate Dean and Director of Urban Health Program. Application for aid should be made upon acceptance.

* member AMCAS

University of Iowa*
College of Medicine
Iowa City, IA 52242

NEW MCAT: required

GPA: 3.6 overall, 3.6 science

FOUNDED 1850; *publicly controlled.*

ENROLLMENT: 470 men, 220 women (total); 120 men, 65 women (first-year).

COSTS: tuition $5200 ($12,800 out-of-state), student fees $100, other expenses $6100.

APPLICATIONS should be submitted between June 15 and December 1; the application fee is $20. Notification begins December 15; response must be received within 2 weeks; $50 deposit needed to hold place in class. Early Decision plan is available. Preference is given to state residents; nonresidents are considered only when applying under the Early Decision plan. Admission factors include GPA (science and overall), New MCAT scores, and personal qualifications as judged from recommendations. *Correspondence to:* Coordinator of Admissions.

MINORITY STUDENTS comprise 9% of the students enrolled, 8% of the first-year class; most of these students receive aid. The $10 application fee may be waived. The College of Medicine sponsors the Educational Opportunity Program, which provides financial and academic assistance for minority and disadvantaged students. A summer program is offered for entering students. *For additional information:* Program Associate for Student Affairs. Applications for aid should be made by March 31.

* member AMCAS

202

University of Kansas*
School of Medicine
39th Street and Rainbow Boulevard
Kansas City, KS 66103

NEW MCAT: required

GPA: 3.7 overall, 3.7 science

FOUNDED 1880 as a two-year institution, introduced four-year program in 1906; *publicly controlled.*

ENROLLMENT: 515 men, 245 women (total); 125 men, 70 women (first-year).

COSTS: tuition $5900 ($12,500 out-of-state), student fees $150, other expenses $5800.

APPLICATIONS should be submitted between June 15 and November 1; the application fee is $15 for non-residents. Notification begins February 1; response must be received within 2 weeks; $50 deposit needed to reserve place in class. Early Decision plan is available. Preference is given to state residents; the class is first filled with kansas residents, after which a few highly qualified nonresidents are accepted. Admission factors weighted most heavily include GPA, New MCAT, premedical advisor's evaluation, interview, performance in required premedical courses, and trends in academic performance. The recruitment program for minorities encourages application from qualified women. *Correspondence to:* Director, Student Admissions and Records.

MINORITY STUDENTS comprise 2% of the total student body, 3% of the first-year class. The $15 application fee for out-of-state applicants may be waived. The School of Medicine sponsors a prematriculation Summer Enrichment Program and an ongoing recruitment program, in addition to its tutorial and counseling programs for matriculated minority students. *For additional information:* Melvin Williams, Director of Affirmative Action. Applications for aid should be made upon acceptance.

* member AMCAS

University of Kentucky*
College of Medicine
Albert B. Chandler Medical Center
800 Rose Street
Lexington, KY 40536

NEW MCAT: required

GPA: 3.5 overall

FOUNDED 1954; *publicly controlled.*

ENROLLMENT: 245 men, 125 women (total); 65 men, 30 women (first-year).

COSTS: tuition $4400 ($15,000 out-of-state), other expenses $9300.

APPLICATIONS should be submitted between June 15 and November 15; there is no application fee. Notification begins August 15; response must be received within 2 weeks; $100 deposit needed to hold place in class. Early Decision plan is available. Preference given to state residents; approximately 90 places in the entering class are reserved for Kentucky residents. Admission factors weighted most heavily include GPA, New MCAT scores, premedical letters of recommendation, extracurricular activities, exposure to medicine, and the personal interview. *Correspondence to:* Admissions, Room MN-104.

MINORITY STUDENTS comprise 3% of the student body, 2% of the first-year class; most of these students receive aid. The College of Medicine sponsors a pre-matriculation program, "Med Prep," in which selected students participate in a one-year academic and work experience in preparation for entering medical school. The office of Special Student Programs maintains recruitment programs for blacks, women, and students from the Appalachian region. Tutorial assistance is available during the academic year. *For additional information:* Associate Dean for Education. Application for aid should be made in April (prior to matriculation).

* member AMCAS

University of Louisville*
School of Medicine
Health Sciences Center
Louisville, KY 40292

NEW MCAT: required

GPA: 3.6 overall

FOUNDED 1833, acquired by state in 1970; *publicly controlled.*

ENROLLMENT: 330 men, 165 women (total); 85 men, 40 women (first-year).

COSTS: tuition $4400 ($16,000 out-of-state), other expenses $9700.

APPLICATIONS should be submitted between June 15 and November 15; the application fee is $15. Notification begins October 1; response must be received within 2 weeks; $100 deposit needed to hold place in class. Early Decision plan is available. Preference given to state residents; 85% of the first-year places are reserved for residents. Admission factors counted most heavily include GPA, New MCAT, motivation and personality as evaluated by interview, and extracurricular activities. *Correspondence to:* Office of Admissions.

MINORITY STUDENTS comprise 4% of the student body, 6% of the first-year class; most of these students are receiving aid. Tutorial assistance is arranged through the Office of Student Affairs for students of disadvantaged backgrounds and who express an interest in securing such help. The $15 application fee may be waived. *For additional information:* Director of Special Programs. Application for aid should be made upon student's acceptance of offer of admission.

* member AMCAS

University of Maryland*
School of Medicine
655 West Baltimore Street
Baltimore, MD 21201

NEW MCAT: required

GPA: 3.6 overall

FOUNDED 1808; *publicly controlled.*

ENROLLMENT: 390 men, 205 women (total); 95 men, 60 women (first-year).

COSTS: tuition $6100 ($12,300 out-of-state), student fees $950, other expenses $8600.

APPLICATIONS should be submitted between June 15 and December 1; the application fee is $25. Notification begins October 15; response must be received within 3 weeks; no deposit needed to hold place in class. Early Decision plan is available. Preference given to state residents. Admission criteria weighted most heavily include GPA, New MCAT, letters of recommendation, and interview. *Correspondence to:* Committee on Admissions.

MINORITY STUDENTS comprise 9% of the student body, 8% of the first-year class; about 90% of these students receive aid; 80% remain to graduate. The $25 application fee may be waived. During the summer prior to acceptance, the School of Medicine, in conjunction with the Johns Hopkins School of Medicine, sponsors COME, a program for disadvantaged and minority students. *For additional information:* Dr. Robert Harrell, Assistant Dean of Student Affairs. Applications for aid are provided upon acceptance, and must be submitted before May 1 (flexible).

* member AMCAS

University of Massachusetts*
Medical School
55 Lake Avenue, North
Worcester, MA 01655

NEW MCAT: required

GPA: 3.5 overall, 3.5 science

FOUNDED 1962, admitted first class in 1970; *publicly controlled.*

ENROLLMENT: 220 men, 185 women (total); 55 men, 50 women (first-year).

COSTS: tuition $5900, student fees $400, other expenses $11,900.

APPLICATIONS should be submitted between June 15 and December 1; application fee is $18. Notification begins October 15; response must be received within 2 weeks; $100 deposit needed to hold place in class. Early Decision plan is available for Massacusetts residents only. Currently, only residents of Massachusetts are considered for admission. Admissions decisions are based on the New MCAT, GPA, letters of recommendation, character, maturity, and motivation. *Correspondence to:* Associate Dean of Admissions.

MINORITY STUDENTS comprise 6% of the total student body; 5% of first-year students. Financial assistance is available; approximately 70% of all students receive aid. *For additional information:* Assistant Dean for Community and Minority Affairs. Application for aid should be made after acceptance.

* member AMCAS

University of Medicine and Dentistry of New Jersey*
New Jersey Medical School
185 South Orange Avenue
Newark, NJ 07103

NEW MCAT: required

GPA: 3.4 overall

FOUNDED 1954, acquired by state in 1965; *publicly controlled.*

ENROLLMENT: 455 men, 235 women (total); 115 men, 75 women (first-year).

COSTS: tuition $8750 ($11,000 out-of-state), student fees $300, other expenses $9100.

APPLICATIONS should be submitted between June 15 and December 15; application fee is $25. Notification begins October 15; response must be received within 2 weeks; $100 deposit needed to hold place in class. Early Decision plan is available. Preference given to state residents. Admission factors weighted most heavily include GPA, MCAT, motivation, determination, recommendations, and extracurricular activities. *Correspondence to:* Director of Admissions.

MINORITY STUDENTS comprise 16% of the total student enrollment, 22% of the first-year class; most of these students receive aid. The $10 application fee and $100 deposit may be waived. The Medical School sponsors a special summer program for minority and disadvantaged students. *For additional information:* Acting Director, Minority Affairs. Application for aid should be made upon acceptance.

* member AMCAS

University of Medicine and Dentistry of New Jersey*
Robert Wood Johnson Medical School
675 Hoes Lane
Piscataway, NJ 08854

NEW MCAT: required

GPA: 3.5 overall

FOUNDED 1966 as a two-year medical school; introduced clinical program for one-half of each class in 1970; in 1974 the school graduated its first class of M.D.'s; formerly known as Rutgers Medical School; *publicly controlled.*

ENROLLMENT: 365 men, 195 women (total); 80 men, 55 women (first-year).

COSTS: tuition $8300 ($10,900 out-of-state), student fees $450, other expenses $8900.

APPLICATIONS should be submitted between June 15 and December 15; application fee is $25. Notification begins October 15; response must be received within 2 weeks; $50 is needed to hold place in class. Early Decision plan is available. Preference is given to state residents; usually nonresidents are limited to between 10% and 20% of each class. Selection factors include academic achievement, MCAT scores, faculty recommendation and the personal interview. *Correspondence to:* Office of Admissions.

MINORITY STUDENTS comprise 10% of the total student body, 11% of the first-year class. The Medical School sponsors a prematriculation summer program for accepted minority and disadvantaged students. *For additional information:* Associate Dean for Student Affairs. Financial aid materials are available upon acceptance.

* member AMCAS

University of Miami
School of Medicine
P.O. Box 016159
Miami, FL 33101

NEW MCAT: required

GPA: 3.5 overall

FOUNDED 1952; *private, state-supported.* A special program enables a person with a Ph.D. degree in science or mathematics to earn an M.D. degree in 2 years.

ENROLLMENT: 430 men, 205 women (total); 95 men, 50 women (first-year).

COSTS: tuition $14,250, student fees $100, other expenses $13,300.

APPLICATIONS should be submitted between July 1 and December 31; the application fee is $50. Notification begins October 15; response must be received within 2 weeks; $50 deposit required to hold place in class. Preference is given to state residents; more than 95% of the students in the most recent first-year class were residents. Admission factors counted most heavily include GPA, New MCAT, faculty evaluations, motivation, and the personal interview. *Correspondence to:* Office of Admissions.

MINORITY STUDENTS comprise 5% of the total student body, 8% of the first-year students; a majority of these students receive aid. A Committee on Minority Affairs is involved in recruitment and assistance to minority students. Tutorial programs are available. The $50 application fee may be waived. *For additional information:* Dr. Robert Bragg, Associate Dean. Applications for aid should be submitted in March.

University of Michigan*
Medical School
1301 Catherine Street
Ann Arbor, MI 48109

NEW MCAT: required

GPA: 3.6 overall

FOUNDED 1850; *publicly controlled.* Combined 7-year program leading to the baccalaureate and M.D. degrees offered.

ENROLLMENT: 535 men, 235 women (total); 145 men, 70
women (first-year).

COSTS: tuition $8500 ($15,000 out-of-state), student fees
$50, other expenses $6100.

APPLICATIONS should be submitted between June 15 and
November 15; the application fee is $20. Notification
varies; response deadline is flexible; $100 deposit
needed to hold place in class. Early Decision plan is
available. Preference is given to state residents. Selection factors include academic achievement, New MCAT
scores, and personal qualifications as judged from the
personal interview, letters of recommendation, and extracurricular activities. *Correspondence to:* Admissions
Office.

MINORITY STUDENTS comprise 5% of the total student body,
8% of the first-year class; most of these students receive
aid. In 1968 the Medical School instituted a decelerated
schedule, the "Flexible Program," in which students of
disadvantaged backgrounds are permitted to complete
the medical school curriculum at a rate geared to the
individual's abilities. The $20 application fee may be
waived. *For additional information:* Assistant Dean for
Student and Minority Affairs. Applications for aid should
be made upon acceptance.

* member AMCAS

211

University of Minnesota—Duluth*
School of Medicine
10 University Drive
Duluth, MN 55812

NEW MCAT: required

GPA: 3.5 overall

FOUNDED 1969; *publicly controlled* two-year basic medical
and clinical sciences school. Upon completion of the
two-year program at Duluth, students transfer to the de-
gree-granting program at the University of Minnesota at
Minneapolis.

ENROLLMENT: 65 men, 30 women (total); 30 men, 15
women (first-year).

COSTS: tuition $6800 ($13,600 out-of-state), student fees
$300, other expenses $5600.

APPLICATIONS should be submitted between June 15 and
November 15; there is no application fee. Notification
begins October 15; response must be received within 2
weeks; $100 deposit needed to hold place in class. Early
Decision plan is available. Strong preference is given to
residents of Minnesota. Residents of certain northern-
most counties of Wisconsin may be accepted. Admission
factors counted most heavily include GPA, New MCAT,
and potential to practice primary care in rural areas or
small towns. *Correspondence to:* Office of Admissions,
Room 107.

MINORITY STUDENTS comprise 3% of the student body, 5%
of the first-year class; all of these students receive aid;
86% remain to graduate. The school sponsors a special
program which offers preparation for health professions
to American Indians at the University of Minnesota's
Duluth and Morris campuses, and Bimidji State College.
For additional information: Admissions Office. Application deadline for aid varies according to specific program applied to.

* member AMCAS

University of Minnesota*
Medical School—Minneapolis
420 Delaware Street, S.E.
Minneapolis, MN 55455

NEW MCAT: required

GPA: 3.5 overall

FOUNDED 1888; *publicly supported.* The flexible program permits completion of the 4-year curriculum in 3 years.

ENROLLMENT: 605 men, 355 women (total); 135 men, 70 women (first-year).

COSTS: tuition $6450 ($13,000 out-of-state), student fees $300, other expenses $5600.

APPLICATIONS should be submitted between June 15 and November 15; there is no application fee. Notification begins October 15; response must be received within two weeks; $50 deposit required to reserve a place in class. Early Decision plan is available. Preference is given to state residents; in recent years, over 90% of the students have been from Minnesota. Admissions decisions are based on the New MCAT, GPA and personal interview as well as the honesty, dedication, and motivation of the applicant. *Correspondence to:* Associate Dean, Admissions and Student Affairs.

MINORITY STUDENTS comprise 3% of the total student body, 1% of first-year students. Financial aid is available. *For additional information:* Assistant to the Dean for Student Affairs. Application for aid should be made after notification of acceptance.

* member AMCAS

University of Mississippi*
School of Medicine
2500 North State Street
Jackson, MS 39216

NEW MCAT: required

GPA: 3.5 overall

FOUNDED 1903 as a two-year school, introduced four-year program in 1955; *publicly controlled.*

ENROLLMENT: 310 men, 105 women (total); 75 men, 30 women (first-year).

COSTS: tuition $6100 ($12,100 out-of-state), student fees $100, other expenses $8000.

APPLICATIONS should be submitted between June 15 and December 1; there is no application fee. Notification begins October 15; response must be received within 2 weeks; $50 ($100 out-of-state) deposit needed to hold place in class. Early Decision plan is available for Mississippi residents only. Preference given to state residents. Admission factors weighted most heavily include GPA, New MCAT, motivation, and the personal interview. *Correspondence to:* Division of Student Services and Records.

MINORITY STUDENTS comprise 7% of the total student enrollment, 10% of the first-year class. The Office of Minority Student Affairs assists with recruitment. *For additional information:* Director of Minority Affairs. There is no deadline for financial aid applications.

* member AMCAS

University of Missouri—Columbia*
School of Medicine
One Hospital Drive
Columbia, MO 65212

NEW MCAT: required

GPA: 3.4 overall, 3.4 science

FOUNDED 1841 as a two-year school, introduced 4-year program in 1955; *publicly controlled.*

ENROLLMENT: 290 men, 135 women (total); 70 men, 40 women (first-year).

COSTS: tuition $6300 ($10,000 out-of-state), student fees $150, other expenses $7100.

APPLICATIONS should be submitted between June 15 and November 15; there is no application fee. Notification begins October 15; response must be received within 2 weeks; $100 deposit needed to reserve place in class. Early Decision plan is available. Preference is given to state residents. Admission criteria include academic performance, New MCAT results, and personal qualifications as evaluated from letters of recommendation, the personal interview, and the formal application. *Correspondence to:* Office of Admissions, MA202 Medical Sciences Building.

MINORITY STUDENTS comprise 4% of the total student body, 2% of the first-year class; most of these students are receiving aid. The School of Medicine sponsors flexible curriculum alternatives and summer enrichment programs for students of disadvantaged backgrounds. *For additional information:* Associate Dean for Student Affairs.

* member AMCAS

University of Missouri—Kansas City
School of Medicine
5100 Rockhill Road
Kansas City, MO 64110

NEW MCAT: not required   ACT: required

FOUNDED 1971; *publicly controlled.* The School of Medicine sponsors only a combined six-year program, in cooperation with the College of Arts and Sciences, leading to the baccalaureate and M.D. degrees.

ENROLLMENT: 200 men, 155 women (total); 45 men, 40 women (first-year).

COSTS: tuition $6500—$7500 ($10,500—$12,500 out-of-state), other expenses $6400.

APPLICATIONS should be submitted between September 1 and January 1; there is an application fee of $50 for non-residents. Notification begins April 15; response must be received within 2 weeks; $100 deposit needed to hold place in class. Residency in Missouri is of prime consideration. Admissions requirements include demonstrated ability to perform on a college level based on a combination of high school rank and scores on a standardized college aptitude test. Personal qualities such as leadership, stamina, reliability, motivation for medicine, and range of interests are also considered. *Correspondence to:* University Admissions Office.

MINORITY STUDENTS comprise 6% of the total student body, 4% of first-year students. There is a variety of aid available to medical students. *For additional information:* Chairman, Minority Recruitment and Retention Committee. Application for aid should be made by January 1.

University of Nebraska*
College of Medicine
42nd Street and Dewey Avenue
Omaha, NE 68105

NEW MCAT: required

GPA: 3.7 overall

FOUNDED 1880; *publicly controlled.*

ENROLLMENT: 310 men, 180 women (total); 75 men, 55 women (first-year).

COSTS: tuition $3500 ($6500 out-of-state), student fees $450, other expenses $9600.

APPLICATIONS should be submitted between June 15 and November 15; there is no application fee. Notification begins January 1; response must be received within 2 weeks; $100 deposit needed to hold place in class. Strong preference is given to state residents; over 95% of a recent freshman class were Nebraska residents. Admission criteria include scholastic record, New MCAT scores, letters of recommendation, and the personal interview. *Correspondence to:* Chairperson, Admissions Committee, Room 5017, Wittson Hall.

MINORITY STUDENTS comprise 6% of the total student body, 7% of first-year students; a majority of these students receive aid. Academic assistance is made available to students who require such help. *For additional information:* Director of Minority Student Affairs. Application for aid should be made by April 1.

* member AMCAS

University of Nevada*†
School of Medicine
Reno, NV 89557

NEW MCAT: required

GPA: 3.3 overall

FOUNDED 1969 as two-year basic science school; in 1977 expanded to a four-year program granting the M.D. degree; *publicly controlled.*

ENROLLMENT: 130 men, 60 women (total); 30 men, 15 women (first-year).

COSTS: tuition and fees $5100 ($12,000 out-of-state), other expenses $8200.

APPLICATIONS should be submitted between June 15 and November 1; the application fee is $35. Notification begins January 15; response must be received within 2 weeks; no deposit needed to hold place in class. Early Decision plan is available for Nevada residents only. Strong preference is given to state residents; 85% of first-year places are reserved for in-state residents. The remaining places are filled with first preference to residents of WICHE states without medical schools (Alaska, Montana, Idaho, and Wyoming), followed by candidates from other WICHE states. Admission factors include GPA, New MCAT scores, college attended, letters of recommendation, and health care experience. *Correspondence to:* Office of Admissions.

MINORITY STUDENTS comprise 2–3% of the total student body. The $35 application fee may be waived. *For additional information:* Associate Dean for Academic and Curricular Affairs. Application for aid should be made after acceptance, prior to May 1.

* member AMCAS
† member WICHE

218

University of New Mexico*†
School of Medicine
Albuquerque, NM 87173

NEW MCAT: required

GPA: 3.4 overall

FOUNDED 1961; *publicly controlled.*

ENROLLMENT: 175 men, 125 women (total); 45 men, 30 women (first-year).

COSTS: tuition $2300 ($6500 out-of-state), student fees $50, other expenses $8300.

APPLICATIONS should be submitted between June 15 and November 15; the application fee is $10. Notification begins March 15; response must be received within 4 weeks; no deposit needed to secure position in class. Early Decision plan is available; nonresidents must apply through EDP. Preference is given to state residents and residents of western states without medical schools (Alaska, Idaho, Montana, Wyoming). Admission factors include academic performance, New MCAT scores, letters of recommendation, and the personal interview. *Correspondence to:* Office of Admissions, Room 107, Basic Medical Sciences Building.

MINORITY STUDENTS comprise 18% of the total student body, 15% of first-year students; most of these students receive aid. The School of Medicine sponsors a special Summer Basic Science Course for minority students of disadvantaged backgrounds, in addition to its recruitment program for such students. *For additional information:* Dr. Alonzo C. Atencio, Assistant Dean, Student Affairs.

* member AMCAS
†member WICHE

University of North Carolina at Chapel Hill*
School of Medicine
Chapel Hill, NC 27599

NEW MCAT: required

GPA: 3.4 overall

FOUNDED 1879, became four-year school 1952; *publicly controlled.*

ENROLLMENT: 380 men, 260 women (total); 105 men, 65 women (first-year).

COSTS: tuition $1300 ($9000 out-of-state), student fees $350, other expenses $5800.

APPLICATIONS should be submitted between June 15 and November 15; the application fee is $35. Notification begins October 15; response must be received by school within three weeks; $100 deposit needed to hold place in class. Early Decision plan is available. Preference is given to state residents; 90% of recent first-year students have been from North Carolina. The percentage of women enrolled usually reflects trends in the distribution of the applicant pool. Selection factors include academic achievement, personal qualifications, and potential for medicine. *Correspondence to:* Registrar, CB#7000 MacNider Hall.

MINORITY STUDENTS comprise 14% of the student body, 18% of the first-year class; most of these students receive aid. The School of Medicine sponsors an elective Summer Medical Sciences Program for minority and disadvantaged students. The Admissions Committee includes both minority students and faculty. *For additional information:* Dr. Marion Phillips, Associate Dean.

* member AMCAS

University of North Dakota
School of Medicine
501 Columbia Road
Grand Forks, ND 58201

NEW MCAT: required

GPA: 3.0 overall (minimum)

FOUNDED 1905 as a two-year basic science school; 1981 introduced a full four-year program; *publicly controlled.*

ENROLLMENT: 135 men, 75 women (total); 30 men, 25 women (first-year).

COSTS: tuition $7000 ($17,000 out-of-state), student fees $250, other expenses $9300.

APPLICATIONS should be submitted between July 1 and November 1; the application fee is $15. Notification begins December 15; response should be received by school within four weeks; $75 deposit needed to hold place in class. Strong preference given to state residents; any remaining places will be filled with preference to residents of neighboring western states without medical schools (Alaska, Montana, Wyoming, and Idaho). Admission criteria include academic record, new MCAT results, letters of recommendation, and the personal interview. *Correspondence to:* Secretary, Committee on Admissions.

MINORITY STUDENTS comprise 8% of the student body, 10% of the first year class; 100% of these students receive aid. The School of Medicine sponsors a special recruitment program, INMED, to encourage applications from American Indians; approximately 5 places in the entering class and reserved for students accepted under this program. *For additional information:* Director, INMED Program. Application for aid should be made upon acceptance.

University of Oklahoma*
College of Medicine
P.O. Box 26901
Oklahoma City, OK 73190

NEW MCAT: required

GPA: 3.5 overall, 3.5 science

FOUNDED 1910; *publicly controlled.*

ENROLLMENT: 420 men, 170 women (total); 100 men, 45 women (first-year).

COSTS: tuition $3250 ($8000 out-of-state), student fees $200, other expenses $8100.

APPLICATIONS should be submitted between June 15 and October 15; the application fee is $10 for residents, $15 for nonresidents. Notification begins October 15; response must be received by school within two weeks; $100 deposit needed to hold place in class. Preference is given to state residents. Admissions decisions based on the New MCAT, GPA, recommendations, and personal interview. *Correspondence to:* Coordinator.

MINORITY STUDENTS comprise 10% of the total student body; 10% of first-year students. A majority of these students receive aid. There are various types of financial aid available; students may apply upon acceptance. *For additional information:* Admissions Coordinator.

* member AMCAS

University of Pennsylvania*
School of Medicine
36th and Hamilton Walk
Philadelphia, PA 19104

NEW MCAT: required

GPA: 3.6 overall, 3.6 science

FOUNDED 1765; *private.*

ENROLLMENT: 430 men, 235 women (total); 110 men, 45 women (first-year).

COSTS: tuition $16,000, student fees $590, other expenses $9800.

APPLICATIONS should be submitted between June 15 and November 1; the application fee is $55. Notification begins December 1; response must be received by school within two weeks; $100 deposit needed to hold place in class. Preference is given to state residents; approximately 50% of a recent entering class were Pennsylvania residents. Admission criteria include performance in academic courses, record of extracurricular activities and community service, New MCAT scores, and character as judged by the Committee on Admissions. *Correspondence to:* Director of Admissions, Suite 100-Medical Education Building.

MINORITY STUDENTS comprise 9% of the total student body, 11% of the first-year class; most of these students receive aid. The $55 application fee (on request) may be waived. *For additional information:* Dr. Helen O. Dickens, Associate Dean for Minority Affairs. Application for aid may be submitted upon acceptance.

* member AMCAS

University of Pittsburgh*
School of Medicine
Pittsburgh, PA 15261

NEW MCAT: required

GPA: 3.5 overall, 3.5 science

FOUNDED 1883; *state-related.*

ENROLLMENT: 380 men, 160 women (total); 100 men, 45 women (first-year).

COSTS: tuition $13,800 ($19,200 out-of-state), student fees $90, other expenses $12,300.

APPLICATIONS should be submitted between June 15 and November 15; the application fee is $40. Notification begins November 15; response must be received within 2 weeks; no deposit needed to hold place in class. Early Decision plan is available. Some preference is given to state residents. Selection factors include scholastic achievement, New MCAT results, letters of recommendation, extracurricular activities, and the personal interview. *Correspondence to:* Office of Admissions, M-245 Scaife Hall.

MINORITY STUDENTS comprise 10% of the student body; about 13% of first-year students. Most of these students receive aid. The $40 application fee may be waived. *For additional information:* Assistant Dean for Student Affairs and Special Projects. Applications for aid may be submitted by accepted students in March.

* member AMCAS

University of Puerto Rico
School of Medicine
G.P.O. Box 5067
San Juan, PR 00963

NEW MCAT: required

GPA: 3.6 overall, 3.5 science

FOUNDED 1950; *publicly controlled.*

ENROLLMENT: 340 men, 215 women (total); 85 men, 55 women (first-year).

COSTS: tuition $2600 ($8100 per semester out-of-state), student fees $250, other expenses $6600.

APPLICATIONS should be submitted between July 1 and December 15; the application fee is $15. Notification begins February 15; response must be received by school within two weeks; $25 deposit needed to hold place in class. Preference is given to residents; a recent class had no members from mainland U.S. or other countries. Admission criteria counted most heavily include GPA, New MCAT, recommendations, personal interview, and extracurricular activities. Application for aid may be made with application for admission or after acceptance. *Correspondence to:* Central Admissions Office.

University of Rochester
School of Medicine and Dentistry
601 Elmwood Avenue
Rochester, NY 14642

NEW MCAT: not required

GPA: not available

FOUNDED 1920; *private.*

ENROLLMENT: 275 men, 145 women (total); 65 men, 35 women (first-year).

COSTS: tuition $16,500, student fees $700, other expenses $7000.

APPLICATIONS should be submitted between June 15 and November 1; the application fee is $50. Notification begins November 15; the response must be received within 2 weeks; no deposit needed to hold place in class. Admission factors weighted most heavily include GPA, with specific emphasis on performance in the natural sciences. Candidates are also expected to provide evidence of a varied background, intellectual curiosity, and demonstrated commitment. *Correspondence to:* Director of Admissions.

MINORITY STUDENTS comprise 8% of the student body, 3% of the first-year class; most of these students are receiving aid. The $50 application fee may be waived. Tutorial assistance and remedial work are provided for all students who exhibit special academic needs. *For additional information:* Associate Dean for Minority Affairs. Application for aid can be made either at the time of application or upon acceptance.

University of South Alabama*
College of Medicine
307 University Boulevard
Mobile, AL 36688

NEW MCAT: required

GPA: 3.5 overall

FOUNDED 1969, accepted first class in 1973; *publicly controlled.*

ENROLLMENT: 165 men, 95 women (total); 40 men, 25 women (first year).

COSTS: tuition $5000 ($10,000 out-of-state), student fees $950, other expenses $6100.

APPLICATIONS should be submitted between June 15 and November 1; the application fee is $25. Notification begins October 15; response must be received within 2 weeks; $50 deposit needed to hold place in class. Early Decision plan is available for Alabama residents only. Preference given to state residents. Admission factors counted most heavily include GPA, New MCAT, premedical advisory committee recommendations, and personal interview. *Correspondence to:* Office of Admissions.

MINORITY STUDENTS comprise 6% of the total student body, 10% of first-year students. The $25 application fee may be waived. *For additional information:* Assistant Dean for Special Programs. Application for aid should be made upon acceptance.

* member AMCAS

University of South Carolina*
School of Medicine
Columbia, SC 29208

NEW MCAT: required

GPA: not available

FOUNDED 1974, first class admitted 1977; *publicly controlled.*

ENROLLMENT: 180 men, 70 women (total); 50 men, 15 women (first-year).

COSTS: tuition and fees $4100 ($8200 out-of-state), other expenses $9600.

APPLICATIONS should be submitted between June 15 and December 1; the application fee is $20. Notification begins October 15; response must be received within 2 weeks; $100 deposit needed to hold place in class. Early Decision plan is available. Preference is given to state residents. Selection factors include academic and personal qualifications. *Correspondence to:* Associate Dean for Admissions.

MINORITY STUDENTS comprise 6% of the total student body, 6% of the first-year class. *For additional information:* Associate Dean for Admissions.

* member AMCAS

University of South Dakota*
School of Medicine
Vermillion, SD 57069

NEW MCAT: required

GPA: 3.5 overall, 3.5 science

FOUNDED 1907 as two-year school, became four-year
school in 1974; *publicly controlled.*

ENROLLMENT: 145 men, 55 women (total); 35 men, 15
women (first-year).

COSTS: tuition $6200 ($12,800 out-of-state), student fees
$950, other expenses $7600.

APPLICATIONS should be submitted between June 15 and
November 15; the application fee is $15. Notification
begins December 15; response must be received by
school within two weeks; $100 deposit needed to hold
place in class. Strong preference is given to state residents; in recent years almost all students have been from
South Dakota. Applicants are selected on the basis of
academic achievement as indicated on all scholastic records, the New MCAT, curiosity, study habits, learning
ability, and fitness for the study of medicine as perceived by their instructors, and estimates of character,
motivation and intellect as observed during the personal
interview. Application for aid is made after fall classes
begin. *Correspondence to:* Office of Student Affairs,
Room 105.

MINORITY STUDENT ADMISSIONS: Minority students comprise
less than 1% of the student body. *For additional information:* Associate Dean, Office of Student Affairs.

* member AMCAS

University of Southern California*†
School of Medicine
2025 Zonal Avenue
Los Angeles, CA 90033

NEW MCAT: required

GPA: 3.6 overall, 3.6 science

FOUNDED 1885, *private*.

ENROLLMENT: 435 men, 160 women (total); 100 men, 40 women (first-year).

COSTS: tuition $11,000, student fees $130, other expenses $7250.

APPLICATIONS should be submitted between June 15 and November 1; the application fee is $50. Notification begins November 15; response must be received within 2 weeks; $100 deposit needed to hold place in class. Early Decision plan is available. Admission factors weighted most heavily include GPA, New MCAT results, extracurricular activities, the personal statement, letters of recommendation, and the interview. *Correspondence to:* Office of Admissions.

MINORITY STUDENTS comprise 5% of the total student body, 9% of the first-year class. The $50 application fee may be waived. The School of Medicine sponsors a Summer Workshop for minority and disadvantaged students, including both academic and hospital orientation programs. Tutorial assistance is available during the academic year. *For additional information:* Althea Alexander, Director, Minority Affairs. Application for aid should be made upon acceptance.

* member AMCAS
†member WICHE

University of South Florida
College of Medicine
12901 Bruce B. Downs Boulevard
Tampa, FL 33612

NEW MCAT: required

GPA: 3.6 overall, 3.6 science

FOUNDED 1965, accepted first class in 1971; *publicly controlled.*

ENROLLMENT: 265 men, 120 women (total); 70 men, 30 women (first-year).

COSTS: tuition $1800 ($4500 out-of-state), student fees $55, other expenses $4500.

APPLICATIONS should be submitted between July 1 and December 1 for residents, until October 5 for nonresidents; the application fee is $15. Notifications begin August 31; response must be received within 2 weeks; no deposit is necessary to hold a place in class. Early Decision plan is available for Florida residents only. Strong preference given to state residents; in recent years all of the entering students have been Florida residents. Admissions criteria include the New MCAT, GPA, letters of recommendation, personal interview, character, and motivation. *Correspondence to:* Admissions Office, Box 3.

MINORITY STUDENTS comprise 2% of the student body, 2% of the first-year class; some financial assistance is available. *For additional information:* Associate Dean for Continuing Medical Education and Affirmative Action Affairs.

University of Tennessee, Memphis
College of Medicine
800 Madison Avenue
Memphis, TN 38163

NEW MCAT: required

GPA: 3.6 overall

FOUNDED 1851; merged with University of Tennessee in 1911; *publicly controlled.*

ENROLLMENT: 490 men, 150 women (total); 100 men, 45 women (first-year).

COSTS: tuition and fees $6200 ($9600 out-of-state), other expenses $6100.

APPLICATIONS should be submitted between June 15 and November 15; the application fee is $25. Notification begins October 15; response must be received within two weeks; $100 deposit needed to hold place in class. Strong preference is given to state residents. Admission factors counted most heavily include GPA, New MCAT, course load and content, extracurricular activities, work experience, personal interview, recommendations, and evaluations. *Correspondence to:* Director of Admissions.

MINORITY STUDENTS comprise 3% of the total student enrollment, 5% of the first-year class; 100% of these students receive aid. The $25 application fee may be waived. *For additional information:* Assistant Dean for Student Affairs. Application for aid should be submitted within 30 days of acceptance.

University of Texas
Southwestern Medical Center at Dallas
Southwestern Medical School
5323 Harry Hines Boulevard
Dallas, TX 75235

NEW MCAT: required

GPA: not available

FOUNDED 1943, acquired by state 1949; *publicly controlled.*

ENROLLMENT: 550 men, 245 women (total); 135 men, 70 women (first-year).

COSTS: tuition $4500 ($18,000 out-of-state), student fees $350, other expenses $12,900.

APPLICATIONS should be submitted between April 15 and October 15. Notification begins January 15; response must be received within two weeks; no deposit needed to hold place in class. Preference is given to state residents; 90% of the places in each class are reserved for Texas residents. Admission factors weighted most heavily include GPA, New MCAT, the personal interview, and preprofessional advisory committee recommendations. All applications are processed by the University of Texas System Medical and Dental Application Center, 210 W. 6th Street, Suite B-41, Austin, TX 78701. The application fee ranges from $35 up ($70 up for nonresidents), depending on number of schools applied to in the University of Texas System. *Correspondence to:* Office of the Registrar.

MINORITY STUDENTS comprise 12% of the total student body, 15% of the first-year class. Tutorial assistants are available for those who require additional academic help. *For additional information:* Assistant Dean for Student Affairs. Application for aid should be made between April 1 and July 1.

University of Texas
Medical School at Galveston
Galveston, TX 77550

NEW MCAT: required

GPA: 3.3 overall

FOUNDED 1881; *publicly controlled.* The School of Medicine offers a three-year program leading to the M.D. degree in addition to the four-year curriculum.

ENROLLMENT: 550 men, 235 women (total); 150 men, 65 women (first-year).

COSTS: tuition $4500 ($18,000 out-of-state), student fees $250, other expenses $8600.

APPLICATIONS should be submitted between April 15 and October 15. Notification begins January 15; response must be received by school within two weeks; no deposit needed to hold place in class. Preference is given to state residents; no more than 10% of the class may be nonresidents. Admission factors counted most heavily include GPA, New MCAT, letters of recommendation and the personal interview. All applications are processed by the University of Texas System Medical and Dental Application Center, 210 W. 6th Street, B-41, Austin, TX 78701. The application fee ranges from $35 up ($70 up for nonresidents), depending on number of schools applied to in the University of Texas System. *Correspondence to:* Office of Admissions, Ashbel Smith Building, Route M-16.

MINORITY STUDENTS comprise 15% of the student body, 20% of the first-year class; most of these students receive aid. The School of Medicine sponsors a Summer Orientation program and an on-going tutorial program for minority and disadvantaged students. A Minority Student Office provides special training and counseling programs. *For additional information:* Director of Office of Special Programs. Application for aid should be made after acceptance.

University of Texas
Medical School at Houston
P.O. Box 20708
Houston, TX 77225

NEW MCAT: required

GPA: 3.5 overall

FOUNDED 1969; *publicly controlled.*

ENROLLMENT: 500 men, 295 women (total); 140 men, 80 women (first-year).

COSTS: tuition $4200 ($16,800 out-of-state), student fees $300, other expenses $7600.

APPLICATIONS should be submitted between April 15 and October 15. Notification begins January 15; response must be received by school within two weeks; no deposit needed to hold place in class. Preference is given to state residents. Selection factors include GPA, New MCAT results, premedical advisory committee recommendations, personal interviews, as well as evidence of leadership and potential for medicine. All applications are processed by the University of Texas System Medical and Dental Application Center, 210 W. 6th Street, Suite B-41, Austin, TX 78701. The application fee ranges from $35 up ($70 up for nonresidents), depending on number of schools applied to in the University of Texas System. *Correspondence to:* Office of Admissions, Room G-024.

MINORITY STUDENTS comprise 10% of the total student body, 10% of the first-year class. *For additional information:* Coordinator of Student Support.

University of Texas
Medical School at San Antonio
7703 Floyd Curl Drive
San Antonio, TX 78284

NEW MCAT: required

GPA: 3.6 overall

FOUNDED 1959, first class matriculated in 1966; *publicly controlled.*

ENROLLMENT: 540 men, 260 women (total); 145 men, 70 women (first-year).

COSTS: tuition $4600 ($18,000 out-of-state), student fees $250, other expenses $13,000.

APPLICATIONS should be submitted between April 15 and October 15. Notification begins January 15; response should be received within 2 weeks; no deposit needed to hold place in class. Preference is given to state residents; the University of Texas System restricts nonresident acceptances to 10% of the freshman class and to students whose qualifications would place them among the top third of entering class. In a recent year, only 7% of the first-year students were nonresidents. Admission criteria include academic background, new MCAT scores, recommendations from premedical advisor, achievements in areas other than academics, maturity, and motivation. All applications are processed by the University of Texas System Medical and Dental Application Center, 210 W. 6th Street, Suite B-41, Austin, TX 78701. The application fee ranges from $35 up ($70 up for nonresidents), depending on number of schools applied to in the University of Texas System. *Correspondence to:* Registrar.

MINORITY STUDENTS comprise 14% of total student enrollment, 14% of first-year students; most of these students receive aid. There are affirmative action programs for the women and minority applicants, students and staff of the Health Science Center. *For additional information:* Associate Dean for Student Affairs.

236

University of Utah*†
School of Medicine
50 North Medical Drive
Salt Lake City, UT 84132

NEW MCAT: required

GPA: not available

FOUNDED 1905 as a two-year school, introduced four-year program in 1943; *publicly controlled.*

ENROLLMENT: 325 men, 75 women (total); 90 men, 10 women (first-year).

COSTS: tuition $4000 ($9000 out-of-state), student fees $350, other expenses $7800.

APPLICATIONS should be submitted between June 15 and October 15; the application fee is $25. Notification begins November 1; response must be received within 2 weeks; $100 deposit needed to hold place in class. Early Decision plan is available; nonresidents must apply through plan. Preference is given to state residents; the college is obligated to have a minimum of 75 Utah residents in the entering class. Approximately one-half of the out-of-state students are residents of western states without medical schools (Alaska, Idaho, Montana, Wyoming). Applicants are considered on the basis of scholarship, evaluation by premedical instructors, New MCAT scores, personality, and motivation. *Correspondence to:* Director, Medical School Admissions.

MINORITY STUDENTS comprise 5% of the total student body, 6% of the first-year class. The $25 application fee may be waived. The Admissions Committee has an active subcommittee on minority admissions recruiting qualified minority students. *For additional information:* Coordinator, Minority Affairs. The school notifies incoming freshmen when it is time to submit applications for aid.

* member AMCAS
†member WICHE

University of Vermont*
College of Medicine
Burlington, VT 05405

NEW MCAT: required

GPA: 3.4 overall, 3.4 science

FOUNDED 1822; *publicly controlled.*

ENROLLMENT: 215 men, 165 women (total); 50 men, 45 women (first-year).

COSTS: tuition $8700 ($19,000 out-of-state), student fees $350, other expenses $8100.

APPLICATIONS should be received between June 15 and November 1; the application fee is $50. Notification begins December 15; response must be received within 2 weeks; $100 deposit required to hold place in class. Preference is given to residents of Vermont, as well as Maine and New York. Admission criteria include GPA, New MCAT, the personal interview, and letters of evaluation from faculty. *Correspondence to:* Admissions Office, Given Building.

MINORITY STUDENTS are encouraged to apply; currently none are enrolled. *For additional information:* Associate Dean for Admissions. Application for aid should be made after acceptance.

* member AMCAS

University of Virginia*
School of Medicine
Box 235
Charlottesville, VA 22908

NEW MCAT: required

GPA: 3.5 overall

FOUNDED 1824; *publicly controlled.*

ENROLLMENT: 385 men, 165 women (total); 90 men, 50 women (first-year).

COSTS: tuition $5700 ($11,750 out-of-state), student fees $600, other expenses $6900.

APPLICATIONS must be received between June 15 and November 15; the application fee is $50. Notification begins October 15; response must be received within 2 weeks; $100 deposit required to hold place in class. Early Decision plan is available. Preference is given to state residents. Admission factors weighted most heavily include the New MCAT, GPA, recommendations, interview, and personal qualities. *Correspondence to:* Office of the Dean—Admissions, Box 235.

MINORITY STUDENTS comprise 5% of the student enrollment, 7% of the first-year class. There are various scholarships and loans available to students. The $50 application fee may be waived. *For additional information:* Assistant Dean.

* member AMCAS

University of Washington*
School of Medicine
Seattle, WA 98195

NEW MCAT: required

GPA: 3.6 overall, 3.5 science

FOUNDED 1945; *publicly controlled.* In 1969 the School of
Medicine introduced the WAMI program, a decentral-
ized curriculum in which students may take part of their
elective phase (third and fourth years) at community
clinical units away from the University.

ENROLLMENT: 435 men, 280 women (total); 95 men, 70
women (first-year).

COSTS: tuition $4100 ($10,500 out-of-state), other expenses
$7800.

APPLICATIONS should be submitted between June 15 and
November 1; the application fee is $35. Notification be-
gins November 1; response must be received within 2
weeks; $50 deposit needed to hold place in class. Pref-
erence is given to residents of Washington and western
states without medical schools (particularly Alaska,
Montana, and Idaho). Candidates are considered com-
paratively on the basis of academic performance, medical aptitude, motivation, maturity, and demonstrated
humanitarian qualities. *Correspondence to:* Committee
on Admissions, Health Sciences Center T-545.

MINORITY STUDENTS comprise 6% of the total student enrollment, 6% of the first-year class. *For additional information:* Director, Minority Affairs Program. Applications for aid should be made after acceptance.

* member AMCAS

240

University of Wisconsin*
Medical School
1300 University Avenue
Madison, WI 53706

NEW MCAT: required

GPA: 3.6 overall

FOUNDED 1907 as a two-year school, introduced four-year
program in 1924; *publicly controlled.*

ENROLLMENT: 410 men, 210 women (total); 89 men, 65
women (first-year).

COSTS: tuition and fees $8400 ($11,600 out-of-state), other
expenses $5200.

APPLICATIONS should be submitted between June 15 and
November 15; the application fee is $20. Notification
begins December 1; response must be received within
2 weeks; no deposit needed to hold place in class. Early
Decision plan is available for Wisconsin residents only.
Preference is given to state residents; a maximum of 5%
of the first-year places are open to nonresidents. Admission factors include academic performance, New
MCAT results, and personal qualifications as judged
from interviews and letters of recommendation. *Correspondence to:* Admissions Committee, Medical Sciences Center, Room 1205.

MINORITY STUDENTS comprise 6% of the total student body,
9% of first-year students; most of these students receive
aid. *For additional information:* Specialist—Student
Services. Applications for aid should be made upon acceptance, prior to February 15.

* member AMCAS

Vanderbilt University*
School of Medicine
21st Avenue South and Garland Avenue
Nashville, TN 37232

NEW MCAT: required

GPA: 3.8 overall, 3.8 science

FOUNDED 1873; *private.*

ENROLLMENT: 285 men, 100 women (total); 75 men, 20 women (first-year).

COSTS: tuition $12,500, student fees $500, other expenses $8200.

APPLICATIONS should be submitted between June 15 and November 1; the application fee is $50. Notification begins October 15; response must be received by school within two weeks; no deposit needed to hold place in class. Early Decision plan is available. Admission factors weighted most heavily include GPA, New MCAT, recommendations, and evidence of motivation. *Correspondence to:* Office of Admissions, 109 Light Hall.

MINORITY STUDENTS comprise 2% of the student body, 1% of the first-year class. The $50 application fee may be waived. The School of Medicine seeks to enroll a diversified entering class and encourages application from women and members of ethnic minority groups currently underrepresented in medicine. *For additional information:* Director, Office of Minority Student Affairs. Application for aid should be made by June 1.

* member AMCAS

242

Virginia Commonwealth University
Medical College of Virginia*
School of Medicine
Box 565
MCV Station
Richmond, VA 23298

NEW MCAT: required

GPA: 3.5 overall, 3.5 science

FOUNDED 1838; *publicly controlled.* The School of Medicine offers the option to earn the M.D. degree in three years.

ENROLLMENT: 440 men, 225 women (total); 105 men, 65 women (first-year).

COSTS: tuition $5800 ($11,800 out-of-state), student fees $550, other expenses $6100.

APPLICATIONS should be submitted between June 15 and November 15; the application fee is $50. Notification begins October 15; response must be received within 2 weeks; $100 deposit needed to hold place in class. Early Decision plan is available. Preference given to state residents; 74% of a recently enrolled class were Virginia residents. Admission factors counted most heavily include GPA, New MCAT, personal characteristics, premedical evaluations, and interviews. *Correspondence to:* Dr. Miles E. Hench, Associate Dean, Admissions.

MINORITY STUDENTS comprise 6% of the student body, 7% of the first-year class; most of these students receive aid. The $50 application fee may be waived. *For additional information:* Associate Dean, Medical School Admissions. Application for aid should be made upon acceptance.

* member AMCAS

Washington University*
School of Medicine
660 South Euclid Avenue
St. Louis, MO 63110

NEW MCAT: required

GPA: 3.7 overall, 3.7 science

FOUNDED 1899; *private.*

ENROLLMENT: 405 men, 145 women (total); 85 men, 40 women (first-year).

COSTS: tuition and fees $14,200, other expenses $7700.

APPLICATIONS should be submitted between June 15 and November 1; the application fee is $45. Notification begins October 15; response must be received within 2 weeks; $100 deposit needed to hold place in class. Admissions decisions are based on the New MCAT, GPA, extracurricular activities, personal interview, motivation, character, and attitude. *Correspondence to:* Admissions Officer.

MINORITY STUDENTS comprise 7% of the total student body; 13% of first-year students. The $45 application fee may be waived. *For additional information:* Dr. Robert Lee, Assistant Dean, Minority Student Affairs. Application for aid may be filed upon acceptance.

* member AMCAS

Wayne State University*
School of Medicine
540 East Canfield
Detroit, MI 48201

NEW MCAT: required

GPA: 3.4 overall

FOUNDED 1868; *publicly controlled.*

ENROLLMENT: 695 men, 340 women (total); 160 men, 105 women (first-year).

COSTS: tuition $5800 ($11,600 out-of-state), student fees $350, other expenses $10,700.

APPLICATIONS should be submitted between June 15 and December 15; the application fee is $25. Notification begins October 1; response must be received within 2 weeks; $50 deposit required to hold place in class. Early Decision plan is available. As a state-supported school, Wayne State gives preference to state residents, but 15% of the freshman class may be nonresidents. Admission criteria include academic record, New MCAT scores, interview, recommendations, and personal character. *Correspondence to:* Director of Admissions.

MINORITY STUDENTS comprise 10% of the total student enrollment, 23% of first-year students; most of these students receive aid. The $25 application fee may be waived. *For additional information:* Counselor, Student Affairs. Application for aid should be made after acceptance.

* member AMCAS

West Virginia University*
School of Medicine
Medical Center
Morgantown, WV 26506

NEW MCAT: required

GPA: 3.6 overall, 3.5 science

FOUNDED 1902 as a two-year school, introduced four-year program in 1961; *publicly controlled.*

ENROLLMENT: 230 men, 100 women (total); 50 men, 35 women (first-year).

COSTS: tuition and fees $2700 ($5000 out-of-state), other expenses $7100.

APPLICATIONS should be submitted between June 15 and December 1; the application fee is $30. Notification begins October 15; response must be received within 2 weeks; $100 deposit needed to hold place in class. Early Decision plan is available for West Virginia residents only. Preference is given to state residents; 90% of a recent entering class were West Virginia residents. Admission factors counted most heavily include GPA, New MCAT, and personal qualifications exhibited through the interview and recommendations. *Correspondence to:* Office of Admissions and Records.

MINORITY STUDENTS comprise 1% of the total enrollment; 1% of the first-year class. The $30 application fee may be waived. *For additional information:* Associate Dean for Student Affairs.

* member AMCAS

Wright State University*
School of Medicine
P.O. Box 927
Dayton, OH 45401

NEW MCAT: required

GPA: not available

FOUNDED 1973; *publicly controlled.*

ENROLLMENT: 245 men, 135 women (total); 50 men, 50 women (first-year).

COSTS: tuition $6700 ($8500 out-of-state), student fees $300, other expenses $11,300.

APPLICATIONS should be submitted between June 15 and November 15; the application fee is $25. Notification begins October 15; response must be received within 2 weeks; no deposit needed to hold place in class. Early Decision plan is available. Preference is given to Ohio residents. Of a recent entering class, 95% were Ohio residents. *Correspondence to:* Office of Student Affairs/ Admissions.

MINORITY STUDENTS comprise 12% of the total student body, 15% of the first-year class. Financial aid is available. *For additional information:* Allen N. Pope, Special Projects Officer.

* member AMCAS

Yale University
  School of Medicine
  333 Cedar Street
  New Haven, CT 06510

NEW MCAT: required

GPA: not available

FOUNDED 1810; *private.*

ENROLLMENT: 290 men, 175 women (total); 65 men, 35 women (first-year).

COSTS: tuition $15,000, student fees $150, other expenses $8100.

APPLICATIONS should be submitted between June 1 and November 1; the application fee is $50. Notification begins in December; response must be received within 3 weeks; $100 deposit is necessary to hold place in class. Early Decision plan is available. Admission decisions are based on the New MCAT, GPA, recommendations of instructors, integrity, common sense, scientific skill, stability, and dedication. *Correspondence to:* Office of Admissions.

MINORITY STUDENTS comprise 11% of the total student enrollment, 8% of the first-year class. A Deferred Tuition Option is available; numerous fellowships, scholarships, and loans are also obtainable. *For additional information:* Admissions Office. Application for aid should be made upon acceptance.

Index to U.S. Medical Schools

Albany Medical College, NY, 121
Albert Einstein College of Medicine (of Yeshiva University), NY, 122
Baylor College of Medicine, TX, 123
Boston University, MA, 124
Bowman Gray School of Medicine of Wake Forest University, NC, 125
Brown University, RI, 126
Case Western Reserve University, OH, 127
Chicago Medical School, The, (University of Health Sciences), IL, 199
City University of New York, The, (Mount Sinai School of Medicine), NY, 160
Columbia University, NY, 128
Cornell University Medical College, 129
Creighton University, NE, 130
Dartmouth Medical School, NH, 131
Duke University, NC, 132
East Carolina University, NC, 133
Eastern Virginia Medical School, VA, 134
East Tennessee State University, (Quillen-Dishner College of Medicine), TN, 135
Emory University, GA, 136
F. Edward Hébert School of Medicine, (Uniformed Services University of the Health Sciences), MD, 183
Georgetown University, DC, 137
George Washington University, The, DC, 138
Hahnemann University, PA, 139
Harvard Medical School, MA, 140
Health Science Center at Brooklyn College of Medicine, (State University of New York), NY, 174
Health Science Center at Syracuse College of Medicine, (State University of New York), NY, 175
Howard University, DC, 141
Indiana University, IN, 142
Jefferson Medical College of Thomas Jefferson University, PA, 143
John A. Burns School of Medicine, (University of Hawaii), HI, 198
Johns Hopkins University, The, MD, 144
Loma Linda University, CA, 145
Louisiana State University, (School of Medicine in New Orleans), LA, 146
Louisiana State University, (School of Medicine in Shreveport), LA, 147
Loyola University of Chicago, (Stritch School of Medicine), IL, 148
Marshall University, WV, 149
Mayo Medical School, MN, 150
Medical School at Galveston, (University of Texas), TX, 233
Medical College of Georgia, GA, 151
Medical College of Ohio, OH, 152
Medical College of Pennsylvania, PA, 153
Medical College of Virginia, (Virginia Commonwealth University), VA, 242
Medical College of Wisconsin, WI, 154
Medical School at Houston, (University of Texas), TX, 234
Medical School at San Antonio, (University of Texas), TX, 235

Medical University of South Carolina, SC, 155
Meharry Medical College, TN, 156
Mercer University, GA, 157
Michigan State University, MI, 158
Morehouse School of Medicine, GA, 159
Mount Sinai School of Medicine of the The City University of New York, NY, 160
New Jersey Medical School (University of Medicine and Dentistry of New Jersey), NJ, 207
New York Medical College, NY, 161
New York University, NY, 162
Northeastern Ohio Universities, OH, 163
Northwestern University, IL, 164
Ohio State University, OH, 165
Oral Roberts University, OK, 166
Oregon Health Sciences University, OR, 167
Pennsylvania State University, PA, 168
Ponce School of Medicine, PR, 169
Pritzker School of Medicine, The, (University of Chicago), IL, 193
Quillen-Dishner College of Medicine, (East Tennessee State University), TN, 135
Robert Wood Johnson Medical School, (University of Medicine and Dentistry of New Jersey), NJ, 208
Rush Medical College of Rush University, IL, 170
Saint Louis University, MO, 171
School of Medicine in New Orleans, (Louisiana State University), LA, 146
School of Medicine in Shreveport, (Louisiana State University), LA, 147
Southern Illinois University, IL, 172
Southwestern Medical School at Dallas, (University of Texas), TX, 232
Stanford University, CA, 173
State University of New York, (Health Science Center at Brooklyn College of Medicine), NY, 174
State University of New York, (Health Science Center at Syracuse College of Medicine), NY, 175
State University of New York at Buffalo, NY, 176
State University of New York at Stony Brook, NY, 177
Stritch School of Medicine, (Loyola University of Chicago), IL, 148
Temple University, PA, 178
Texas A&M University, TX, 179
Texas Tech University, TX, 180
Thomas Jefferson University, (Jefferson Medical College), PA, 143
Tufts University, MA, 181
Tulane University, LA, 182
Uniformed Services University of the Health Sciences (F. Edward Hébert School of Medicine), MD, 183
Universidad Central del Caribe, PR, 184
University of Alabama, AL, 185
University of Arizona, AZ, 186
University of Arkansas, AR, 187
University of California, Davis, CA, 188
University of California, Irvine, CA, 189
University of California, Los Angeles, CA, 190
University of California, San Diego, CA, 191
University of California, San Francisco, CA, 192
University of Chicago, (The Pritzker School of Medicine), IL, 193
University of Cincinnati, OH, 194
University of Colorado, CO, 195
University of Connecticut, CT, 196
University of Florida, FL, 197
University of Hawaii, (John A. Burns School of Medicine), HI, 198
University of Health Sciences, (The Chicago Medical School), IL, 199
University of Illinois, IL, 200
University of Iowa, IA, 201
University of Kansas, KS, 202
University of Kentucky, KY, 203
University of Louisville, KY, 204
University of Maryland, MD, 205
University of Massachusetts, MA, 206
University of Medicine and Dentistry of New Jersey, (New Jersey Medical School), NJ, 207
University of Medicine and Dentistry of New Jersey, (Robert Wood Johnson Medical School), NJ, 208
University of Miami, FL, 209
University of Michigan, MI, 210
University of Minnesota, Duluth, MN, 211

University of Minnesota, Minneapolis, MN, 212
University of Mississippi, MS, 213
University of Missouri, Columbia, MO, 214
University of Missouri, Kansas City, MO, 215
University of Nebraska, NE, 216
University of Nevada, Reno, NV, 217
University of New Mexico, NM, 218
University of North Carolina at Chapel Hill, NC, 219
University of North Dakota, ND, 220
University of Oklahoma, OK, 221
University of Pennsylvania, PA, 222
University of Pittsburgh, PA, 223
University of Puerto Rico, PR, 224
University of Rochester, NY, 225
University of South Alabama, AL, 226
University of South Carolina, SC, 227
University of South Dakota, SD, 228
University of Southern California, CA, 229
University of South Florida, FL, 230
University of Tennessee/Memphis, TN, 231
University of Texas, (Southwestern Medical School at Dallas), TX, 232
University of Texas, (Medical Branch at Galveston), TX, 233
University of Texas, (Medical School at Houston), TX, 234
University of Texas, (Medical School at San Antonio), TX, 235
University of Utah, UT, 236
University of Vermont, VT, 237
University of Virginia, VA, 238
University of Washington, WA, 239
University of Wisconsin, WI, 240
Vanderbilt University, TN, 241
Virginia Commonwealth University, (Medical College of Virginia), VA, 242
Wake Forest University, (Bowman Gray School of Medicine), NC, 125
Washington University, MO, 243
Wayne State University, MI, 244
West Virginia University, WV, 245
Wright State University, OH, 246
Yale University, CT, 247

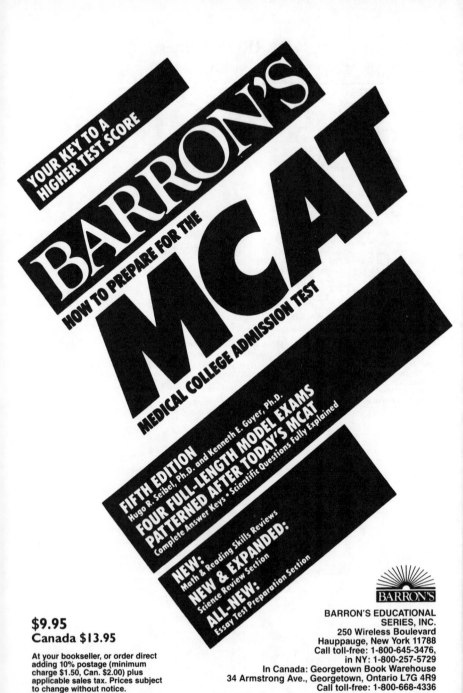

More selected BARRON'S titles:

DICTIONARY OF FINANCE AND INVESTMENT TERMS
John Downes and Jordan Goodman
Defines and explains over 2500 Wall Street terms for professionals, business students, and average investors.
Paperback $8.95, Canada $11.95/ISBN 2522-9, 495 pages
"This is an invaluable fog-cutter for investors."
—*William S. Rukeyser, Managing Editor, FORTUNE Magazine*

DICTIONARY OF REAL ESTATE TERMS
Jack P. Friedman, Jack C. Harris, and Bruce Lindeman
Defines over 1200 terms, with examples and illustrations. A key reference for everyone in real estate. Comprehensive and current.
Paperback $8.95, Canada $11.95/ISBN 3898-3, 224 pages

REAL ESTATE HANDBOOK
Jack P. Friedman, Jack C. Harris, and Bruce Lindeman
A dictionary/reference for everyone in real estate. Defines over 1500 legal, financial, and architectural terms.
Cloth $19.95, Canada $27.50/ISBN 5758-9, 700 pages

HOW TO PREPARE FOR REAL ESTATE LICENSING EXAMINATIONS-SALESPERSON AND BROKER, 3rd EDITION
Jack P. Friedman and Bruce Lindeman
Reviews current exam topics and features updated model exams and supplemental exams, all with explained answers.
Paperback, $9.95, Canada $13.95/ISBN 2996-8, 340 pages

BARRON'S FINANCE AND INVESTMENT HANDBOOK
John Downes and Jordan Goodman
This hard-working handbook of essential information defines more than 2500 key terms, and explores 30 basic investment opportunities. The investment information reflects new Federal Tax Act provisions effective in 1987. Cloth $21.95, Canada $29.95/ISBN 5729-5, 864 pages
"...an excellent investment guide...almost any serious investor will want this book."—*Christian Science Monitor*

BARRON'S FINANCIAL TABLES FOR BETTER MONEY MANAGEMENT
Stephen S. Solomon, Dr. Clifford Marshall, and Martin Pepper
Pocket-sized handbooks of interest and investment rates tables used easily by average investors and mortgage holders. Paperback
Savings and Loans, $5.50, Canada $7.95/ISBN 2745-0, 272 pages
Real Estate Loans, $5.50, Canada $7.95/ISBN 2744-2, 336 pages
Mortgage Payments, $5.50, Canada $7.95/ISBN 2728-0, 304 pages
Stocks and Bonds, $5.50, Canada $7.95/ISBN 2727-2, 256 pages
Comprehensive Annuities, $5.50, Canada $7.95/ISBN 2726-4, 160 pages
Canadian Mortgage Payments, Canada $8.95/ISBN 3939-4, 336 pages
Adjustable Rate Mortgages, *Jack P. Friedman and Jack C . Harris*
$5.50, Canada $7.95/ISBN 3764-2, 288 pages

All prices are in U.S. and Canadian dollars and subject to change without notice. At your bookseller, or order direct adding 10% postage (minimum charge $1.50, Canada $2.00), N.Y. residents add sales tax.

Barron's Educational Series, Inc.
250 Wireless Boulevard, Hauppauge, NY 11788
Call toll-free: 1-800-645-3476, in NY 1-800-257-5729
In Canada: Georgetown Book Warehouse
34 Armstrong Ave., Georgetown, Ontario L7G 4R9